W9-ANH-072

Veronica's Room

BY IRA LEVIN

Plays

Veronica's Room
Dr. Cook's Garden
Drat! The Cat!
Critic's Choice
General Seeger
Interlock
No Time for Sergeants
(from the novel by Mac Hyman)

Novels

The Stepford Wives
This Perfect Day
Rosemary's Baby
A Kiss Before Dying

VERONICA'S ROOM

A MELODRAMA
by Ira Levin

RANDOM HOUSE / NEW YORK

Library of Congress Cataloging in Publication Data

Levin, Ira.
Veronica's room.

Play.
I. Title.
PS3523.E7993V4   1974   812'.5'4   73-20597
ISBN 0-394-49145-9

Manufactured in the United States of America
24689753

VERONICA'S ROOM *was first presented on October 25, 1973,*
by Morton Gottlieb at The Music Box Theatre in New
York City with the following cast:

(*In order of appearance*)

THE WOMAN	Eileen Heckart
THE MAN	Arthur Kennedy
THE GIRL	Regina Baff
THE YOUNG MAN	Kipp Osborne

Directed by   Ellis Rabb
Scenery by   Douglas W. Schmidt
Costumes by   Nancy Potts
Lighting by   John Gleason

The Scene

The play is set in a room in a house about half an hour's drive from Boston. The time is an evening in spring.

ACT ONE: Susan
ACT TWO: Veronica

ACT ONE

Susan

A WOMAN *and a* MAN *come into a dim, sheet-shrouded room. In its lighted doorway, a* GIRL *stands waiting. A* YOUNG MAN *stands behind her. The* WOMAN *and the* MAN *move familiarly among the sheeted shapes, the* WOMAN *lighting a wall bracket and a lamp, the* MAN *partly raising a window without drawing its pale breeze-stirred curtain. The* GIRL *comes into the room, looking about with interest as the* WOMAN *uncovers and lights another lamp. The* YOUNG MAN *follows the* GIRL; *he too looks about, but with an air of misgiving. The* MAN *lights a wall bracket. The* WOMAN *lights a hanging glass-shaded lamp over a round table.*

The room is a bed-sitting room in a turn-of-the-century Victorian house, ornate and somewhat ominous. The door is large and solid. The bed, a single one, is in an angled alcove. A window in the wall beyond it is lightly curtained like the other window. There are doors to a closet and a bathroom. Later the room will be seen to be feminine and attractive within the framework of its heavy architecture. Its decor is of the 1930's, though most of the furniture is a generation older. A chaise longue, the round game table, a desk before the window, a Victrola next to the desk, an artist's easel, a dresser, chairs, bookcases, etc.—all sheeted now.

The WOMAN *and the* MAN *are pleasant looking, in their early or middle sixties. The* WOMAN *is neatly and plainly dressed, the* MAN *a bit rumpled in a worn blue suit. The* GIRL *is twenty, slim and engaging, with long straight hair.*

3

She wears flared pants, a heavy turtleneck sweater, several necklaces. The YOUNG MAN, *stocky and in his late twenties, has a bushy mustache and wears old sports clothes.*

The WOMAN *lifts the cover carefully from the game table, on which lies a partly completed wooden jigsaw puzzle.*

WOMAN (*She has a slight brogue*)   Here's the puzzle she was workin' on, *exactly as she left it.* "Hunters in the Black Forest" is the name of it. Eight hundred pieces. And no picture on the box for assistance! (*The* GIRL *comes closer to the table. The* MAN *is uncovering the desk. The* YOUNG MAN *wanders over to look briefly at a painting on the wall*) She did two or three of these a month, and just before Christmas, Mr. Brabissant would take all the ones she'd done the year before— they were kept in that chest on the landin'; did y' notice the oak chest there?

GIRL   Yes, I did.

MAN   That's a val'able antique, that chest is.
(*He too has a slight brogue*)

WOMAN   And he would give them—give all of them puzzles costin' *ten and twelve dollars each*—to the Walpole firemen, to give to the children. She didn't like to do one she'd done before. A new one was like a new world to move into, she used to say. And of course . . . (*A tender smile*) . . . they *did* indulge her in that.

GIRL   They knew she was going to die?

WOMAN   Oh yes, oh yes. There was no hope at all in those

days. Not for bad cases like hers. *They* knew it, and *she* knew it too, from when she was fifteen years old.

GIRL   Oh wow. (*Looking at the* YOUNG MAN)   It must be awful, knowing it, at that age. Ooh!
(*She winces and shudders; the* YOUNG MAN *nods. The* GIRL *looks again at the* WOMAN, *who is gathering the dust cover together*)

WOMAN   She never let it get her down though. Used to sit here hummin' a melody, happy as could be.

MAN (*Lighting a lamp on the desk*)   Susan dear, if you'd look over here . . . This is where she made the pins and bracelets we told y' about. (*The* GIRL *goes toward the desk. The* YOUNG MAN *moves toward the game table, hands in pockets, looking about. The* WOMAN *puts the dust cover aside*) All her tools, her silver wire, bits of colored glass . . . Here's a pin she made just a day or two before. (*Giving it to the* GIRL) Just look at that work, will y'?

GIRL   Wow, this is *beautiful!* Larry, come look!
(*She holds the pin in the lamplight. The* YOUNG MAN *goes toward her. The* WOMAN *begins uncovering a bookcase*)

MAN   She made bracelets, earrin's, all kinds of things.

GIRL (*Shows the pin to the* YOUNG MAN)   Isn't it beautiful?

YOUNG MAN (*Looks, nods*)   Yeh, it is. It really is.

GIRL (*Taking an arm's-length look*) She could sell these on the street today and make a *fortune!*
(*Gives the pin back to the* MAN)

WOMAN Here's some of her books and magazines . . . There are more by the bed, her favorite ones. And these are her paintin' things. She did that castle there. From her imagination, believe it or not; not copyin' anythin'.
(*The* GIRL *goes toward the painting on the wall*)

YOUNG MAN Did she do anything else, like make ships in bottles?
(*He has a Massachusetts accent. The* WOMAN *looks sharply at him*)

MAN Ah well, she had a lot of time to fill, y' know, stuck in the room here seven whole years.

GIRL (*Looking at the painting*) What sign was she born under? (*Turning, looking at the* WOMAN) Do you know?

WOMAN Sign?

GIRL You know, of the zodiac. Gemini, Capricorn . . .

WOMAN (*Thinks for a moment*) June eighth was her birthday . . .

GIRL That's Gemini. That's *my* sign. I'm June thirteenth.
(*A pause, the* WOMAN, *the* MAN, *and the* YOUNG MAN *looking at the* GIRL)

MAN Well now. Isn't *that* a coincidence . . .

6

(*Another pause, the* GIRL *uncomfortable, having been reminded of something*)

WOMAN   Everythin' is how it was. Her clothes are in the closet, her comb and brush and all are in the bathroom. There's a half-done paintin' on that easel there . . . The Brabissants wouldn't change a *thing*, rest their souls. After she died they used to come in here almost every evenin' and just sit for a while, her over there and him over here, not sayin' *anythin'*. I had to keep the room as clean as any of the others.

MAN   I had to keep the trees by the window cut back, like as if she still needed the light to paint by!

WOMAN   Oh, they adored that girl . . . And John and I did too.

MAN   She used to wave to me when I was workin' this side of the house, as cheerful as if—as if she'd never even *heard* of TB, as if it was someone's *initials* or somethin'!

GIRL (*Looking about approvingly*)   It was lovely of them to keep everything . . . Like making a *shrine*.

YOUNG MAN   *I* don't think it was lovely. I think it was— unhealthy. (*The* GIRL *looks at him with curiosity, the* WOMAN *and the* MAN *resentfully*) I'll bet this is why— (*A movement of his head toward the door*)—Cissie wound up the way she is.

MAN   Oh no, no, no, no, no. Cissie was *always* the—(*A*

waggle of fingers near his temple)—peculiar one of the three.

GIRL   But maybe Larry's right. If the room had been changed, had been *used,* if—Veronica's things had been put away, maybe it would have been easier for Cissie to, you know, *understand.* This must have just *reinforced* everything.

WOMAN   You've got it all *wrong,* dear. She *did* understand, in the beginnin'. It's only these past few years, when she's near dyin' herself, that she's come to think Veronica's alive.

MAN   She's *gone back in time,* that's what Cissie's done. She's in 1935 now; Veronica's alive, *she's* goin' to the Boston Secretarial School—she does her shorthand every night, mind y'!—and Conrad's in his room at the end of the hall.

WOMAN   The three of them was close as fingers.

GIRL   Where's Conrad really?

WOMAN   He died in World War Two. In Japan.

MAN   Lieutenant in the Air Force. That was what finished the Brabissants, him gettin' killed. First their oldest was taken, and then their youngest . . .
    (*A pause, the* WOMAN, *the* MAN *and the* YOUNG
    MAN *watching the* GIRL, *who remembers again
    that she has a decision to make*)

WOMAN   Will y' do it, Susan? Please? It'll make Cissie so happy.

MAN It'll only take half an hour or so, and then I'll drive y' right back to town! You'll still have plenty of time for your walk by the river, and the—(*Winks at the* YOUNG MAN)—moon'll be nice and high to shine on y'! (*To the* GIRL *again*) What d'y' say, dear? Will y'?

WOMAN Y' see the way the room is; we only have to take off the rest of the covers.

GIRL (*Looks indecisively at the* YOUNG MAN, *and at the* WOMAN *again*). I—don't know . . .
      (*The* WOMAN *and the* MAN *look anxiously at each other*)

YOUNG MAN Does she *really look* that much like Veronica?

WOMAN Oh Lord, yes!   MAN She could be her *twin* practically! I never *seen* anythin' like it!

WOMAN When the two of y' came into that restaurant I thought I was seein' a *ghost*, so help me! (*To the* GIRL) And the more so, the closer y' got.

MAN I thought Maureen was havin' a stroke or somethin'! I had me back to y', remember, and didn't see till y' sat down. (*To the* WOMAN) Remember, dear, I grabbed your hand and asked if y' was all right? (*To the* YOUNG MAN) I really thought the old girl was dyin' on me! (*Looking at the* GIRL) And then *I* saw . . . Oh yes, she really looks that much like Veronica. Enough to fool *anyone*, not just poor Cissie.

GIRL   You said you'd show us a picture.

WOMAN   That's right, of course; go get it, John. Sneak in there without wakin' her. The big one the photographer took. *You* know. (*The* MAN *goes out*) She's got 'em all lined up, on the mantel and the tables; pictures of all of 'em. (*Moves closer to the* GIRL) You'll see. It's yourself, standin' right here, with your hair brought back and gathered behind—(*Taking the* GIRL's *hair in both hands, arranging it*)—and a nice bright smile on your face. There . . . (*Bites her lip, awed*) Oh Lord, seein' y' in this room of hers, it scares the daylights out of me!
 (*She lets go of the* GIRL's *hair and moves away, rubbing her hands distressfully. The* GIRL, *combing down her hair with her fingers, looks helplessly at the* YOUNG MAN, *and at the* WOMAN *again*)

GIRL   I guess I have a common face. There was a girl back home who looked like me. (*To the* YOUNG MAN) She was a year ahead of me, in school I mean, and kids were always stopping me and asking me about assignments I never heard of! (*To the* WOMAN's *back*) And the same thing used to happen to her.

YOUNG MAN   Did you ever purposely trick anyone?

GIRL   No. But we could've, if we'd wanted to. We weren't friends though. She was kind of a creep. (*Smiles at him*) Gorgeous, but kind of a creep.

WOMAN (*Turning to the* GIRL)   Are you *sure* no part of your family's from here?

GIRL   Positive. My parents were born in Ohio, and my grandparents are from Poland and Germany.

WOMAN (*Throwing off her discomfort*) Well, maybe over there then; who knows? Mr. Brabissant's folks were from Belgium originally. All them places are in there together, aren't they?
(*The* GIRL *nods, smiling*)

YOUNG MAN It's a continent, Mrs. Mackey. It's pretty big.
(*The* MAN *comes in, a small framed picture in his hand*)

MAN She's up, workin' on her *shorthand*. (*Closes the door most of the way. To the* WOMAN) Didn't even know we was back. (*To the* GIRL) I couldn't think of an excuse for the big one, but I sneaked this one out. (*Gives the picture to her*)

WOMAN Oh that's no good! She's twelve or thirteen in that one!

MAN I couldn't pick and choose, Maureen; it was nearest me hand.
(*The* YOUNG MAN *joins the* GIRL *looking at the picture. The* WOMAN *goes to them*)

WOMAN There. And that's Cissie and Conrad. and *Mrs.* Brabissant. On the swing on the porch. It's gone now.

GIRL She does look like me at that age . . . Except for the braces. On me I mean, not her.

YOUNG MAN Braces?

GIRL On my teeth.

11

YOUNG MAN   Oh.

WOMAN   She had lovely teeth. Nice and straight.

GIRL   So did I, but my father's a dentist.
(*Looks for another moment, then makes sure the* YOUNG MAN *is through and gives the picture to the* WOMAN)

WOMAN   Later on, while Cissie's in *here,* John'll go in and get the *good* picture. We'll show it to y' after.

YOUNG MAN   Now just a second; Susan hasn't said she's going to do it.

WOMAN   Oh y' must, Susan! Please! All she keeps sayin', mornin' and night, is "Why is Veronica angry with me? Why won't she let me come visit no more?"

MAN   The doctor says she felt *guilty when Veronica died.* Sometimes a child'll *do* that, he says, even when it's natural causes. And now she's a child again, eighteen in her head, not—fifty-six or whatever.

WOMAN   We're askin' so little of y'. Y' put on a dress, y' pin back your hair. Y' say "Hello, Cissie, I'm glad you're lookin' so well. No, I'm not angry with y', Cissie, it's just I don't want y' to catch the TB." It's so little, and it'd be such a blessin' for her.

GIRL   I'm—not sure it's a good thing to do.

MAN   What are y' talkin' about?   WOMAN   How could it *not* be, when it's the one thing she's longin' for?

GIRL (*Gathers her thoughts*) Look, I—I know you *mean* well, and you think we'd be doing her a favor . . . But—I've studied some psychology. I'm a *sociology major*. It's not good to—play along with somebody's delusions. It just makes them *more* dependent on—

WOMAN (*Interrupting her*) She's *dyin'*, Susan! She is *dyin'*! Didn't we make that clear in the car? She's *dyin'* of cancer! It's too *late* to get rid of her delusions! All we can do now is—make her a little *happy* when we've got the chance!
> (*Upset, she turns from the* GIRL, *moves to the game table and puts the picture down on it. The* MAN *touches the* GIRL's *shoulder gently*)

MAN A few weeks is all she's got. A month or two at the most. That's quotin' the doctor now. (*The* GIRL *looks at the* YOUNG MAN; *he shakes his head doubtfully, rubbing the back of it. The* MAN *looks angrily at him*) What are your objections, Larry? Perhaps you'll tell us.

WOMAN (*Having steadied herself, she turns to the* GIRL) Susan . . . We've never gone to that restaurant before. We go to a place on State Street, where John has a cousin who's a waiter. Tonight, walkin' from the parkin' lot, I suddenly felt we should go someplace different this week. Don't ask me why 'cause I don't know. "Let's go in *there*," I says to John, "it'll be a change." "We'll have to tip," says John. "What the hell," says I . . . So in we go. And five minutes later *you and Larry come in*. And sit down next to us. Now don't you think—that someone, somewhere, was guidin' our steps tonight? *Your* steps, *our* steps? Puttin' us together so we could do this kind thing for Cissie?

YOUNG MAN Making us not have any plans for the evening?

WOMAN Yes! Even that! Maybe even that. Yes!
(*Pins him with an angry stare, then looks at the* GIRL *for her answer*)

GIRL Could Larry and I talk together please? Just for a minute or two?
(*The* WOMAN *stays looking at her*)

MAN Sure y' can. Of course. (*Taking the* WOMAN's *arm*) Come on, Maureen, let's let 'em talk it over. (*The* WOMAN *lets the* MAN *take her toward the door*) We'll look in on Cissie. Y' can't blame 'em for hesitatin', dear. It's not everyone that wants to involve themselves in— oops! (*About to draw the door closed, he leaves the* WOMAN *outside it and goes quickly to the game table and takes the picture. He smiles apologetically on his way back to the* WOMAN) Better slip this back before she misses it; eyes like a hawk! Come on, dear.
(*He draws the door closed. The* GIRL *looks at it for a moment, and turns to the* YOUNG MAN)

GIRL She *is* dying, and it *would* make her feel better . . .

YOUNG MAN Oh, I *guess* so . . . But maybe they've got other reasons. Did you think of that?

GIRL What do you mean? *What* other reasons?

YOUNG MAN (*Crossing the room*) Well . . . it's not hard to imagine some . . .

GIRL It's hard for *me* to. Like what?

YOUNG MAN (*Turns to face her*) All right, the parents
are dead, right? Mr. and Mrs. Brabissant?

GIRL Yes.

YOUNG MAN And Veronica's dead, and Conrad is dead
. . . (*The* GIRL *nods*) Only Cissie is alive, and she's
dying. (*The* GIRL *looks at him*) Maybe she knows something, where some money is hidden, or—some papers or
something, and *she'll tell Veronica,* but she won't tell—
(*A thick brogue*)—the kindly old family servants, bless
their darlin' shamrock hearts! (*The* GIRL *stares at him*)
It's possible, isn't it? Or maybe they want her to sign
something.

GIRL Man, you really *are* a lawyer, aren't you!

YOUNG MAN Did you think I wasn't?

GIRL Well, guys bullshit. (*Moves toward him*) You
don't *look* like one, with that mustache.

YOUNG MAN It's fake. I take it off before I go into the
courtroom.

GIRL *All* they want me to *say* is that I'm not *angry* with
her.

YOUNG MAN That's all they've told you *so far.* Maybe
they'll have some other suggestions later on. (*The
brogue again*) "An' by the way, dear, would y' ask her
t' tell y' where she's hidin' the old lady's *joolery*?"

GIRL   Shhh! Not so *loud* . . .

YOUNG MAN   You're right; they're probably listening.

GIRL   Oh man. Look, if you're so suspicious *now,* how come you were so *un*suspicious in the restaurant? I don't remember you kicking me under the table or anything.

YOUNG MAN   We were just going to go look at a picture; they weren't saying anything then about—you putting on an act. (*The* GIRL *moves away from him*) And I was afraid if I said no, you'd think I was in too much of a hurry to get down to the river.

GIRL   Oh great. (*Turns to him*) I was afraid you'd think *I* was in too much of a hurry!
      (*They look at each other. He smiles*)

YOUNG MAN   I guess we should have been more open.

GIRL   (*Looking around dispiritedly*)   You can say *that* again . . . (*Decides, and looks at him*) I'm going to do it. I am. It'll be fun. I was Cordelia in *King Lear.*

YOUNG MAN   High school?

GIRL   (*Nods*)   It'll be a good deed too. If they tell me to ask her anything, I just *won't,* that's all.

YOUNG MAN   I . . . *guess* they're on the level. They could twist her arm and *make* her tell, if there was something she was—keeping from them.

GIRL   Do you *always* mistrust people? I hope not. Oh wow, they forgot about my voice; what if I don't *sound* right?

YOUNG MAN   You must or they wouldn't think you could do it.

GIRL   I can do a Baaston aaccent. For a few minutes, at least.

YOUNG MAN   Can you keep from saying "oh wow"?

GIRL   Oh wow. Oh—something. What did they *say* in 1935?

YOUNG MAN (*Shrugs*)   I don't know. Boop-boop-a-doop.

GIRL   Oh wow. *Ooh!*
(*She slaps her forehead, and winces and smiles at him. He smiles at her*)

YOUNG MAN   Should I call the leprechauns?

GIRL (*Raises her hand*)   No, wait a minute. (*Moves closer to him, and stands before him*) Touch me. (*He looks at her, not moving*) You haven't touched me yet, do you know that? I mean not even my elbow crossing the street. Let alone my more interesting features.

YOUNG MAN   It's—only our second date.

GIRL   Our first. Sunday doesn't count.

YOUNG MAN   So?

GIRL *Touch* me; I'm promiscuous. (*He touches her shoulder, and withdraws his hand. She looks feelingly at him*) She really bugged you, didn't she. That *mother* of yours, I mean. You're very uptight.

YOUNG MAN (*Uncomfortably*) No I'm not . . . Jesus Christ, we're in a house out past Walpole, in a room covered with sheets, where a dead girl did jigsaw puzzles—all right, yes, I'm uptight! . . . I'll touch you later. Everywhere.

GIRL (*Smiles at him*) Okay. (*Goes toward the door, and turns and looks back at him*) If not, we'll just talk! (*She opens the door and calls into the hallway*) You can come in now! (*She smiles at the* YOUNG MAN. *The* MAN *and the* WOMAN *come in. The* GIRL *nods happily to them*) I'll *do* it!

WOMAN (*Claps her hands*) Oh thank y', darlin'! (*Hugging the* GIRL) Bless y'! You're an angel!

MAN I knew y' would! I knew it all along! I just now made a dollar bet with her; "She'll *do* it," I said. "She has a *warm* heart!" (*Snaps his fingers at the* WOMAN) Come on, Maureen, pay up! Come on, come on, where's me dollar? Hand it over.

WOMAN (*Waving her hand at him*) Oh shut up, you and your bets.
    (*Moves to the door*)

MAN You're welshin' on me? (*To the* GIRL) Y' see what she is? She's a welsher! (*To the* WOMAN) Come on now, Maureen! Y' made a bet, y' gotta—

WOMAN (*Her back to the door, closing it; interrupting him*) Shut up, John. (*The* MAN *falters to silence. The* WOMAN *looks steadily at him*) We've got to get the covers off, and Susan fixed up.
(*A pause. The* MAN *nods*)

MAN Of course, of course . . .

GIRL Can I help? With the covers, I mean.
(*The* MAN *goes toward the bed*)

WOMAN Of *course* y' can, dear! The more *hands* there is, the less *work* there is! Get that one there.
(*She begins gathering the cover from a chair. The* GIRL *moves to the desk chair*)

GIRL Oh listen, is my *voice* all right? Do I *sound* like Veronica?

WOMAN Y' do near enough! The sight of y' 'll be so perfect, I'm sure Cissie won't pay much mind to the sound!

MAN (*Gathering the bed's dust cover*) Her hearin' ain't that good anyway; it's her eyes that're sharp, not her ears.
(*The* GIRL *begins gathering the desk chair's cover. The* YOUNG MAN, *having been looking on with an air of lingering disapproval, turns and begins gathering the cover from the dresser. The* WOMAN *puts her cover on the chaise*)

WOMAN Put 'em all on the chays here; then we'll bundle 'em up in the one.

GIRL   I can do a Boston accent a little; should I? Veronica must have had one.

WOMAN   Yes, that'd help y' sound right . . .
 (*Takes the cover from a side table*)

GIRL (*Putting her cover on the chaise*)   I'll paak my caa in Haavaad Yaad.
 (*She starts toward the Victrola as the* YOUNG MAN *brings his cover to the chaise*)

WOMAN   We're grateful to y', Larry, for lettin' Susan *do* the favor for us.

GIRL (*Turning*)   Letting me? He didn't *let* me; I make my *own* decisions.
 (*The* YOUNG MAN *goes around the game table*)

MAN   Oho, so you're a liberated woman, are y'!

GIRL   Bet your—*life* I am.

YOUNG MAN (*Taking the cover from the chair before the puzzle*)   How come I paid for dinner?

GIRL (*Taking the cover from the Victrola*)   Because *you* asked. When *I* ask, *I'll* pay.

MAN (*To the* YOUNG MAN; *bringing the bed's cover to the chaise*)   I'da paid if y'da let me.

GIRL   Hey, what *is* this?

WOMAN (*Picking up the desk's dust cover from the floor*) The Victrola.

MAN Record player, phonograph.

GIRL Oh wow. (*Turning to the* WOMAN) Hey, that's something else: what did Veronica say instead of "oh wow" and "oh man" and things like that?

WOMAN (*Takes the cover from the* GIRL's *hands and brings it with her own to the chaise; considers as she puts them down*) I believe she kept silent . . .
(*The* GIRL *is given pause. The* YOUNG MAN *smiles, gathering another cover. The* MAN *is uncovering a bookcase on the far side of the bed. The* GIRL *opens the Victrola's top, looks inside, twists her head*)

GIRL "Shuffle Off to Buffalo" . . .

WOMAN (*Gathering a cover*) Oh, that was real popular then. It must have been the last record she played . . . Tsk-tsk.
(*Shakes her head and sighs*)

GIRL Does this work? Can we hear it?

WOMAN I guess it does; try it and see.

MAN (*On his way to the chaise*) Y' wind it on the side there, the handle.

YOUNG MAN We want to get this over with, don't we?

GIRL (*Winding the Victrola*) I want to hear it; it'll help me get in the mood.
(*The* YOUNG MAN *gives an Oh-God look. The* MAN, *having put his cover on the pile, reaches for*

the ones the YOUNG MAN *holds. The* GIRL *fiddles in the Victrola's top)*

WOMAN   John, get the one off the mirror there.

GIRL   It's turning, but the arm doesn't move.

WOMAN   Y've got to do it   MAN   Just pick it up and
yourself.   set it down there.

GIRL   Oh. (*Doing it*) That's not very handy . . .
(*We hear a 1933 or '34 recording of "Shuffle Off to Buffalo," with vocal. While the record plays, the restoring of the room is completed. The* MAN *and the* YOUNG MAN *gather the last of the dust covers, while the* WOMAN *sets out various decorative objects that she takes from drawers in tables and the dresser. The* GIRL *helps some, but her interest is mainly in the song. "Oh, I've heard this!" she says after a few bars, and she hums along and sings, "Off we're gonna shuffle, shuffle off to Buffa-lo," sharing her enjoyment with the others in looks and smiles. The* MAN, *enlisting the* YOUNG MAN's *help—"Gimme a hand here, will y'?"—encloses the heap of dust covers in the cover of the chaise; he carries the bundle from the room—the* YOUNG MAN *opens the door for him and closes it after him— and he returns a few moments later with a towel which he brings into the bathroom. The* WOMAN *gives various instructions throughout: "This goes on the night table. John, get a towel from the closet! Will y' put these on the bookcase there?" etc. As the record nears its end, the room looks warm, attractive and thoroughly lived-in. Another*

lamp may have been lighted, or secondary bulbs in the lamps already lit. The only jarring note is the unfinished painting on the easel, an agony of twisted tree branches, bare and black. The GIRL *becomes aware of it, and moves from the Victrola to stand before it. The* MAN, *watching her from the side of the chaise where he sits resting, sings along with the final "Off we're gonna shuffle, shuffle off to Buffa-lo!" The* YOUNG MAN, *leaning against the dresser with his arms folded, watches him. The* WOMAN, *at the side of the Victrola, lifts its arm, switches it off, and closes its cover*)

YOUNG MAN They don't write them like that any more.

MAN (*Turning to him*) Ain'it the truth! The *junk* they call *songs* now! Honest to God!
(*The* GIRL *doesn't turn. The* WOMAN *watches her, and looks uncomfortably at the painting*)

WOMAN She was—kind of downhearted at the end, I guess.

GIRL That's not *downhearted*, ooh, that's—*anguished*. Ooh!
(*Turns from the painting wincing and hugging her arms*)

MAN Well, y' can't blame her, poor thing, knowin' what was ahead.

WOMAN (*With a hand movement*) Turn it around, John; Cissie may not like it. (*An inviting gesture to the* GIRL) Come on, dear. Now that the *room* is fixed up, it's *your* turn! (*She goes to the closet. The* MAN *rises*

23

and starts toward the easel, watching as the WOMAN
*opens the closet. It's filled with colorful garments, most
of them light and silken, and a rack of shoes hangs on
the door. The* GIRL *approaches slowly. The* WOMAN
*takes out an attractive 1930's-style dress on its hanger,
and another one)* This here is one she liked a lot, and
this here one too. (*Displaying them both*) What d'y'
like, dear? Choose. Whichever y' want.

GIRL (*Looks, and turns coolly to the* YOUNG MAN) I did
not, you will notice, say "oh wow." (*He smiles. The*
GIRL *turns to the closet*) I sure *felt* like it though . . .
(*The* MAN *carefully turns the easel and painting
around to face the wall, while the* GIRL *separates and
looks at the garments in the closet*) It's like the Walpole
branch of Paraphernalia!

WOMAN Of what?

GIRL This boutique in Cambridge that has all kinds of
marvelous far-out things. (*Takes a dress out and in-
spects it at arm's length*) You know my poncho? That's
where I got it.

WOMAN Oh. (*The* GIRL *goes before the mirror over the
dresser and holds the dress against herself*) I was won-
derin' . . .

GIRL It's Peruvian. Shepherds wear them.
(*Takes one of the dresses from the* WOMAN *and
compares it with the other she's holding*)

WOMAN Well, these are what Veronica wore. Which'll
it be?

GIRL (*Shows them to the* YOUNG MAN; *moves toward him*) Which do *you* like?

YOUNG MAN The one that goes on and off the quickest.

GIRL (*Makes a face at him and goes back to the* WOMAN) *This* one.

WOMAN I'da chose it too! It's a good color for y'.
(*She takes the other dress from the* GIRL)

MAN Well. I guess it's time for Larry and me to be gettin' out.

GIRL (*To the* YOUNG MAN) Sorry about that.
(*The* WOMAN *is hanging away the unchosen dresses. The* YOUNG MAN *stands straight*)

YOUNG MAN Can I come back and watch from somewhere, while Cissie is here?
(*The* WOMAN *turns from the closet; she and the* MAN *look at the* YOUNG MAN)

MAN Oh no.   WOMAN No, y' can't do
                                        that.

MAN There's no place to watch from.
(*The* YOUNG MAN *starts to gesture toward the bathroom*)

WOMAN She's liable to want to *use* the bathroom.

MAN She goes a hell of a lot.
(*A pause*)

WOMAN   And she might even want to—see somethin' in the closet. No, I really don't see how y' can—

MAN   (*Interrupting her, beckoning to the* YOUNG MAN) Susan'll tell y' the whole story! Come on, I'll make y' comfortable downstairs. I'll even give y' a sip of Irish whiskey, what d'y' say to that?

YOUNG MAN   (*Going to him*) Oh faith an' begorrah, that'll be a treat. (*The* MAN *laughs. The* YOUNG MAN *looks across the room at the* GIRL. *She waves her fingers at him; he smiles*) Have fun.

GIRL   I expect to. It's a bigger part than Cordelia.

WOMAN   Have y' acted in plays?

GIRL   In high school.

WOMAN   Oh, *that'll* help us . . .
      (*The* YOUNG MAN *goes to the* GIRL, *looks at her, and puts his hand to her cheek. She smiles at him, and puts her hand to his cheek. The* WOMAN *watches, surprised. The* YOUNG MAN *turns and goes back to the* MAN, *who, opening the door, throws a fatherly arm about the* YOUNG MAN's *shoulders*)

MAN   Come along, son, and I'll show y' where there's a nice comfortable chair in front of a TV set!
      (*They go out, the* MAN *drawing the door almost closed after them. The* GIRL's *smile lingers, as does the* WOMAN's *puzzlement*)

26

WOMAN   Y' belong to a *lodge* or somethin'?

GIRL   (*Turns to her with a broader smile*)   No. He's—
shy about touching me.

WOMAN   Oh. (*A glance toward the door*) He seems to
be gettin' over it.

GIRL   (*Nods*)   I think he will. (*Taking the hanger from
the dress she holds*) He had this awful rejecting mother.
She told him right to his face that she never wanted
him.
　　(*Gives the hanger to the* WOMAN)

WOMAN   Oh dear.

GIRL   She probably never touched *him*, so now *he* can't
touch. At least not easily.

WOMAN   (*Hanging the hanger in the closet*)   Can that
be?

GIRL   Oh yes. Yes . . . (*undoing the back of the dress*)
Kids should be touched like crazy. All the time.

WOMAN   (*A pair of shoes in her hands*)   Can y' wear
size—(*Looks in them, squints*)—seven B?
　　(*Goes to the* GIRL)

GIRL   (*Takes them, looks*)—I guess so. I may *moan* a little.

WOMAN   (*Smiling*)   It won't be for long. (*Fixes the* GIRL *with a frank, steady, moment-of-truth gaze)* Y're not wearin' a brassiere, are y'.

GIRL   God no! Nobody does.

WOMAN   Speak for yourself. *(Turns to the dresser, opens a drawer)* Y' better have one with that; it's kind of clingy. Are y' wearin' stockin's?

GIRL   No.

WOMAN *(Finding them in the drawer)*   Stockin's . . . Garters . . .

GIRL   *Garters?*

WOMAN *(Turns and looks at her)*   Y' ain't goin' to keep 'em up by prayin' *(Turns back to the drawer)* A slip . . . Here's a nice slip for y' . . . *(Looking at the* GIRL *again)* Y' are wearin' *pants* . . . *(The* GIRL *nods)* Saints be praised. *(Turning, she tucks the handful of lingerie into the crook of the* GIRL's *arm)* Now go on in there and put 'em on. I'm goin' to dust around a little. *(The* GIRL *goes into the bathroom)* Oh, wait a minute, there's a belt that goes with that dress. Go ahead, I'll get it for y'. *(Turns to the dresser, closes the open drawer, opens another, lifts out a skein of belts)* Narrow satin belt . . . Here it is. *(Puts the others in the drawer, closes it, and brings the belt to the bathroom doorway)* Here y' are.

GIRL *(Taking it)*   Thanks.
    (The WOMAN *closes the door partway, and standing in the lee of it, draws a neckchain from her*

dress. Taking in her hand something attached to the chain, she lifts it off over her head)

WOMAN   Have y' known Larry long?

GIRL *(Off)*   No, we just met Sunday.

WOMAN *(Trying to open the chain, and having difficulty)* Y' seem to know a lot about him.

GIRL *(Off)*   I'm good at drawing people out. And picking up clues.

WOMAN   Clues? What d'y' mean?
    (Uses her teeth on the clasp)

GIRL *(Off)*   Oh, like the fact that he's got a big mustache and short hair. That means that he's *trying* to be open and self-accepting, but part of him is still kind of closed and defensive.

WOMAN *(She has the chain open now and is drawing it up from the object in her hand)*   Oh, that's *interestin'* . . . Can y' do that with everybody?

GIRL *(Off)*   More or less, when I'm not all wrapped up in *myself*.

WOMAN *(Tucking the chain in a pocket and going toward the door to the hall)*   My oh my, you're a very smart girl!
    (Standing before the almost-closed door, she draws it to her and puts the object, a key, into the

outside of it. She tries it; the bolt, a large one, slides smoothly out and in)

GIRL *(Off)*   Mrs. Mackey?

WOMAN   It's Maureen, dear! Call me Maureen!
(Puts the door as it was, leaving the key in it, and moves away)

GIRL *(Off)*   I ought to know more about people and things that Cissie is liable to mention. Who was Veronica's doctor, for instance?

WOMAN *(Looking critically at the chaise)*   Dr. Simpson, that was. He was everybody's doctor, the whole family's.
(Moves the chaise a little farther away from the lamp table by it)

GIRL *(Off)*   Simpson?

WOMAN   That's right. And there was a cook then named Henrietta, with a little boy Morgan who used to hang around and make a pest of himself.
(Adjusts the position of a decorative pillow on the chaise)

GIRL *(Off)*   Were there any friends or relations?

WOMAN *(Taking a handkerchief from a pocket, moving about flicking it at various surfaces, blowing dust from things)*   None that Cissie's likely to mention. The Brabissants was above most of the folks around here, and they weren't that close with their families neither. *He* hated hers and *she* hated his. From what I seen at the funerals they were *both* of them right. (*She flicks and blows. The* GIRL *comes out of the bathroom, fastening the belt of the mid-calf-length dress; it's quite becoming to her*) Oh isn't that nice now!

GIRL   It fits perfectly.

WOMAN (*A small pause*)   I knew it would; you're just the right size.

GIRL   Even the shoes are all right. Either my *feet shrank* or they made sizes bigger in those days. (*Takes a heavy bracelet from her wrist and smiles at the* WOMAN, *who stands looking at her*) What do we do with my hair?

WOMAN (*Looks for another moment*)   I don't suppose y'd —let me cut a little, would y'?

GIRL   Oh no. No. No way.

WOMAN   Well, we'll just have to make it *look* shorter, then. (*Pocketing her handkerchief, going toward the bathroom*) Sit down, I'll get pins.
       (*The* GIRL *moves toward the desk. The* WOMAN, *passing her with a touch on the arm, goes into the bathroom. The* GIRL *puts her bracelet on the corner of the desk and sits in a chair*)

GIRL   If she notices I'll just say I'm letting it grow. She hasn't *seen* Veronica in a long time. I mean even by *her* standards.

WOMAN (*Off*)   That's right; it'll be fine, don't worry. I pay too much mind to little details; John's always tellin' me that. (*Comes out of the bathroom shaking dry a*

comb. She gives the GIRL *a handful of hairpins)* Hold
these and give 'em to me, all right?

GIRL   Sure.
    (*During the following, the* WOMAN *combs the*
    GIRL'*s hair back loosely over her ears and pins it up
    at the back of her neck in as close an approxima-
    tion of a 1930's hairdo as she can manage. The*
    GIRL *hands back pins when the* WOMAN *reaches or
    asks for them)*

WOMAN   I rinsed the comb . . .

GIRL   It was clean; I saw it. The whole bathroom is.

WOMAN   Oh, I come in and clean around once in a
while . . .
    (*A moment of silence, the* WOMAN *working with
    great concentration. The* GIRL *puts her hand to her
    mouth and coughs. Another moment goes by)*

GIRL   Was that all right?

WOMAN   Was *what* all right?

GIRL   My cough.

WOMAN   Oh! Oh *yes*, that was very good, very good.
Just like hers. That was very good . . . Real little
actress . . .
    (*Another pause, the* WOMAN *working, the* GIRL
    thinking)

GIRL   How come Veronica wasn't in a sanitorium? The

Brabissants could have afforded it, couldn't they? This *house*, and all the *land* . . .

WOMAN   Oh yes, they were *loaded*. He had a big mill over in East Walpole. Textile mill. Even in the Depression they were sittin' pretty.

GIRL   Then why didn't they send her—

WOMAN (*Interrupting her*)   Well y' see, it was that they *loved her so much*; they couldn't bear to have her away from them.

GIRL   But wouldn't she have lived longer, in a place like in *The Magic Mountain?* A sanitorium in the Alps . . .

WOMAN   May*be*; I don't know. All I know is they kept her here . . . (*Another pause, the* GIRL *thinking, and looking down at herself uneasily*) Another . . .
        (*The* GIRL *puts a pin in the* WOMAN's *hand*)

GIRL   Maureen?

WOMAN   Mm?

GIRL   These clothes, and the room and all; it's—safe, isn't it? (*The* WOMAN *looks at her, suddenly wary. The* GIRL *turns*) There's no danger of—

WOMAN (*Understanding, relieved*)   Oh of *course* it's safe, darlin'! The whole room was fumigated and all the clothes was taken out and cleaned! No, no, no, no, don't worry about *that!* Of *course* it's safe! I wouldn't be in here meself if there was any danger, would I? Oh no, no, no. Everythin' was cleaned and made all right again. (*She comes around in front of the* GIRL, *lifts the* GIRL's *chin, and looks judiciously at one side of her head and the other*) And germs don't live thirty-five, forty years anyway, do they?

GIRL   I don't know; I don't *think* so . . .

WOMAN (*Fixing a strand of the* GIRL's *hair*) No, I'm *sure* they don't. Everythin's clean; don't you worry. Tell me, d'y' have any brothers and sisters?
       (*Going around in back again*)

GIRL   One brother

WOMAN   Older or younger?

GIRL   Older. He's in Portugal. Wait till I write him about—oh wow! Wait till I tell my *roommates*! They're going to think I made the whole thing up!

WOMAN   *Are* they? Oh, they wouldn't doubt your—

GIRL (*Interrupting her*)   Fact, absolute *fact*! This *one*, Diane, is the complete skeptic! I tell her I found a *penny on the sidewalk*, she doesn't believe me!

WOMAN   Oh my goodness . . .

GIRL   You're going to have to give me a *note* or something, some kind of *proof* that this whole thing *happened*.

WOMAN (*Smiling at her, leaning close to share a secret*) It's *fun* dressin' up and playin' a part, isn't it?

GIRL (*Nods, smiling*) Yes, it is. At least when there's a good reason for doing it.

WOMAN Mmm, yes!

GIRL You can rationalize it then; otherwise it's just—kid stuff. But kid stuff's *okay* once in a while; I don't think people ought to *not* allow themselves to—
(*A knock at the door stops her*)

MAN (*Off*) It's me. Can I come in?

WOMAN Yes, come on in, John! (*The* MAN *comes in and closes the door at his back. He looks at the* WOMAN, *and at the* GIRL, *admiringly*) We're just finishin'.

MAN You're Veronica. As God is me judge!
(*The* GIRL *smiles, pleased*)

WOMAN Doesn't she look grand?

MAN Marvelous, marvelous!

GIRL What's Larry doing?

MAN Watchin' TV. A basketball game.

GIRL Oh? Who's playing.

MAN Didn't notice.

WOMAN Go and get her things out of the bathroom.
(*The* MAN *goes to do so. The* WOMAN *tells the* GIRL) In case Cissie goes in there. I'll put 'em in the linen closet.

GIRL   Is Cissie her real name?

WOMAN   Cecilia.

GIRL   Oh.

WOMAN   There. That looks right enough. (*The* GIRL *rises, touching her hair tentatively. The* WOMAN *smiles and mock-curtsies*) Please don't bother to tip me, miss.

GIRL (*Smiling*)   Okay, I won't. (*She goes and looks at herself in the dresser mirror. The* WOMAN *watches her happily. The* MAN *comes out of the bathroom with the* GIRL's *clothes over his arm, her shoes and necklaces in his hand; he too watches her*) It's nice. I like it! (*Turning to them*) Can I go show Larry?

WOMAN   Oh no, what if she sees y' out of the room?

MAN   I'll bring him up after the *performance*; y' can give him an *encore*.

GIRL (*Smiling*)   Okay. (*Hugs her arms, rubs them*) "Performance" is right; I've got goosebumps!

MAN   Ah, it'll be a breeze! Don't worry about it!

WOMAN (*Putting a chair in its proper position*)   Just say you're not angry with her. I won't let her stay more 'n two minutes.

GIRL   You'll stay here *with* us, won't you? In case she—

WOMAN (*Over her*)   Oh sure I will.

GIRL —says anything I don't understand? Asks a question I can't answer?

WOMAN I'll be *right here*. I'll tell her the doctor says y' mustn't talk too much. And let's turn off a light or two, to make it even *more* convincin'.
(*Turns off the lamp by the chaise*)

MAN (*Turning off the desk lamp*) Eyes like a hawk, she's got.

GIRL (*Standing by the game table; to the* WOMAN) How old is *Conrad*?

WOMAN (*Turning off the wall bracket*) You're twenty, she's eighteen, Conrad is seventeen. (*The* MAN *turns off the other bracket. The* WOMAN *moves near the door and takes a final satisfied look at the* GIRL *and the room. The* MAN *joins her*) Well, I guess we're about ready now, don't y' think?

MAN (*Looks, considers*) Yes . . . I'd say we was all set.

GIRL (*With a relieved smile*) Larry thought you would tell me to *ask* Cissie something.

WOMAN What d'y' mean? MAN Ask her somethin'?

GIRL Where *money* is hidden or something like that.

WOMAN Oh for goodness' sake.

MAN Is *that* why he was against your doin' it?
(*The* GIRL *nods; they shake their heads*)

37

WOMAN Tsk!   MAN Oh my . . .

GIRL   I guess lawyers become suspicious of people.

WOMAN Sure they do, from bein' amongst *lawyers* so much!

GIRL (*Smiling*) He changed his mind, so don't tell him I told you.

MAN (*Raises his right hand*) He'll never know.
      (*Opens the door partway*)

WOMAN It's goin' to take us a couple of minutes to get her ready; she'll want to fix herself up and all.

MAN   We'll hurry her along as much as we can.

WOMAN You make yourself at home. (*Going to the desk*) Do some work on the puzzle there. (*Picking up the* GIRL's *bracelet*) Or look at a book, or play some records.

GIRL   Are you kidding? I'm going to *rehearse*!
      (*The* MAN *opens the door wide; the* WOMAN *waves a hand at the* GIRL *and goes toward it*)

WOMAN Ah, y' don't need to! You're perfect, y' couldn't be better!
      (*She goes out past the* MAN. *He stands looking amiably at the* GIRL, *her clothes over his arm*)

MAN   No, you're right, Susan. You rehearse a little. (*Conspiratorially, with a wink*) Practice bein' Veronica!

(*He goes out and draws the door closed. After a moment the bolt is heard striking home. The* GIRL's *smile gives way to an uncertain frown. She crosses the room, tries the door, and sure enough it's locked*)

GIRL Mr. Mackey? Maureen? (*Listens, hears nothing, and calls louder*) Mr. *Mackey?* John? (*She's puzzled. She stands for a moment, thinking, and then—what can she do?—shrugs her puzzlement off and moves into the room. She wanders thoughtfully, touching the back of the chaise, the edge of the Victrola, picking up one of Veronica's mementos, examining it, putting it down. She turns, faces the door, and smiles warmly*) Hello, Cissie! Oh, it's so good to see you! You're looking—(*It's awful; she throws it away with both hands and girds herself for another try*) Hello, Cissie! You look maavelous! Angry? *Me?* With *you?* Oh Cissie, how could you think—Hel*lo*, Cissie! Oh, I'm *so* glad to see you! (*Coughs*) Angry? With *you?* Oh *no*, dear, it's all **Dr.** *Simpson's* fault! He's such—(*Coughs*) He's such an old *fusspot* about keeping me *isolated!* Conrad hasn't been allowed in either, not for months! (*Not bad; with a tentative nod of approval, she moves toward the door and sings to it, throwing her arms open*)

Hello, Cissie!
Well, hello, Cissie!
    (*Moves about, and sings slowly*)
It's so nice—
    (*Touches something*)
—to have you back—
    (*Turns, taking in the whole room*)
—where you belong . . .

(*She continues a slow humming of "Hello, Dolly!"
moving about, looking, touching. The end of the
first part of the song finds her next to the game
table. She stops and looks down at the puzzle. She
picks up a piece, looks at it, looks at the puzzle, and
sees where the piece goes. She pops it in, surprised
and pleased with herself*)

Ha! (*She picks around at some of the other pieces, and
sits down and studies the puzzle. The curtain of the
partly raised window wafts and falls back. Moonlight
has printed a black silhouette on the curtain: the window sashes and, overlying them, a barred grillwork that
covers the whole of the window. The same shadow pat-
tern is on the curtain of the window beyond the bed.
The* GIRL *picks up the open box of the puzzle and rum-
mages through the pieces. She finds a likely one and
tries it in various places in the puzzle. She begins humming again—"Shuffle Off to Buffalo" in a quick perky
tempo. She sings*)

> Ooooh, ooh, ooh.
> Off we're gonna shuffle,
> Shuffle off to Buffa-lo.

(*She hums the next few bars and sings again*)

> Oooh, ooh, ooh.
> Off we're gonna shuffle,
> Shuffle off to Buffa-lo.

(*She hums the bridge, working at the puzzle—and
stops short as the doorbolt clicks. She rises and
readies herself, watching the door. It opens and the*
WOMAN *comes in holding a glass of milk on a plate.
She seems taller than before. Without looking at
the* GIRL, *she brings the milk to the table by the*

chaise. The GIRL *peers into the dimness, and glances at the open door)* Is she coming? *(The* WOMAN, *having put the milk down, lights the lamp on the table and stands looking at the* GIRL. *She has changed her clothes and her hair style and looks now like a woman of the 1930's—and considerably younger than she looked before. The* GIRL *stares at her)* Hey, you look *terrific!* I didn't know *you* were going to change too.

WOMAN   What are you talking about?
(Her brogue is gone)

GIRL *(An uncertain pause)* What do you mean, what am I talking about? You—changed your dress, your hair . . . You look twenty years younger! *(The* WOMAN, *with an annoyed headshake, turns and goes toward the door)* Is she coming?

WOMAN *(Turns and looks at the* GIRL) Is *who* coming?

GIRL   Cissie. *(The* WOMAN *stares angrily at her. The* GIRL *is unsure whether to laugh or not)* Are you—all right? Don't you remember? *(The* WOMAN *keeps staring at her)* You and *Mr.* Mackey are bringing *Cissie* in. To *see* me. That's why I'm dressed up.

WOMAN *(Looks down at her hands and rubs them, trying to decide how best to cope with this; looks at the* GIRL *with controlled hostility)* Now look, Veronica . . . *(The* GIRL *stands motionless, looking at the* WOMAN, *who goes on—with a Massachusetts accent)* This is *not* the night to give us any trouble, do you understand? Conrad's in bed with a fever of one hundred and one degrees. It's Maureen's night off. And the men at the mill started a sit-down strike today and your father's *not happy* about it. So just drink your milk, and get undressed, and go to bed. Good night.

(*She goes out and closes the door. The bolt clicks. The* GIRL, *staring, moves a few steps toward the door. She turns, and looks at one of the windows with its grillwork-shadowed curtain. She turns farther, and looks at the other window. She turns all the way around, looking at the room and the closed door—fearfully, incredulously. The curtain falls*)

ACT TWO

Veronica

The room is as it was before; the GIRL *is at the closed door, hitting it with her fists.*

GIRL *Unlock this door! Let me out of here! Unlock this goddamn door, God damn it!* (*She takes one of her shoes off, and holding it by the instep, hammers at the door with its high heel*) *Larry? Come up here! Larry!* (*She stops and listens, then hammers again*) LARRY! LARRY! (*She stops and listens, then crouches and puts her eye to the keyhole. She straightens, drops the shoe, and stamps on the floor with her shod foot several times. She listens, and hears nothing. She looks at the door, thinking, and at the desk, and at the bookcase. Taking her other shoe off, she drops it and goes quickly to the bookcase. She searches among art supplies and finds a large sketch pad. Opening it, she tears a sheet from it, drops the pad, and returns to the door. Crouching, she slides the paper under it. She puts it partway through and moves it against the jamb, below the keyhole. Rising, she goes to the desk and looks among the tools there. She comes back to the door holding a small pair of thin long-nosed pliers. Crouching again, she looks into the keyhole, then puts the pliers into it and tries to work the key out on the other side. She stops and withdraws the pliers, looks down, and watches the end of the paper vanish under the door. She rises, and stands facing the door*) Put the key back in and unlock this door.

MAN (*Off*) Move away, Veronica.

45

GIRL   I'm not Veronica; I'm Susan.

MAN (*Off*)   Move away and we'll come in.

GIRL   Get Larry up here.

MAN (*Off*)   Move *away*. (*The* GIRL *stays there, but after a moment she withdraws a few steps*) Further. (*She withdraws farther, and stands watching the door. The key and the bolt are heard, and the door opens. The* MAN *and the* WOMAN *come in. The* MAN *moves a step or two toward the* GIRL; *the* WOMAN *stays by the open door. The* MAN *wears the vest and trousers of a 1930's business suit, with a white shirt and a loosened necktie. Like the* WOMAN, *he looks younger and more authoritative than he did before. Toying with the key in his hand, he looks disapprovingly at the* GIRL, *and down at the shoes on the floor before him. He moves one with the toe of his own shoe, and looks at the* GIRL *again*) Now what's all this banging and screaming about? Hm? (*And he too speaks with a Massachusetts accent, not a brogue. The* GIRL *looks warily at him*) Well, young lady? What do you think you're doing?

WOMAN   Being her miserable *self*, that's what she's doing. (*The* GIRL *looks at the* WOMAN, *and at the* MAN *again. He puts the key into a vest pocket*)

MAN   Well? I'm waiting for an answer.

GIRL   I want to go now. Bring me my clothes.

WOMAN   *Speak in your regular voice!*

GIRL (*Looks at her for a moment*)   I'm speaking in it.

It's—shaking a little, but this is it. (*To the* MAN) Bring me my clothes, please.

MAN (*Tries to make sense of that, but can't*) You're *wearing* them. (*She looks at him. He points*) Well, look. That's not—*nothing!* It's a *dress,* stockings . . .

GIRL (*As loud as she can, moving toward the open door*) *LARRY!*
    (*The* WOMAN *slams the door and stands against it. The* MAN *blocks the* GIRL, *thrusting her back a step with a push at her shoulder. She drops the pliers*)

MAN Don't you raise your voice again! You hear me? You shout like that again and I'll—I'll really give it to you! You hear me? (*The* GIRL *withdraws another few steps, watching him and rubbing her shoulder*) You can talk any which way you like, but you're not going to *shout* any more!
    (*He picks up the pliers. The* WOMAN, *with a sigh, moves from the door*)

WOMAN Anything to torment us, anything to make trouble . . .
    (*She picks up the shoes; the* MAN *tosses the pliers to the desk*)

MAN (*To the* WOMAN) Go downstairs; I'll see that she goes to bed.

GIRL Get Larry up here . . .

MAN (*Turning angrily to her*) Who are you *talking* about? *What* Larry? Larry *Porcelli,* at the *mill?*

47

GIRL   The Larry who's downstairs! Larry Eastwood! The man I came here with! (*The* MAN, *nonplussed, looks at the* WOMAN; *she's seething. The* GIRL *cries at her*) *You just closed the door so he wouldn't hear me!*

WOMAN   I closed the door because *Conrad* is *sleeping!*

GIRL   *Conrad is DEAD!* . . . Now *stop* it! This is *now,* this is 1973. You *know* it is.

WOMAN   Oh Lord!
(*The* MAN *stands staring at the* GIRL)

GIRL   Get my clothes and let me out of here.
(*A pause, the* MAN *and the* WOMAN *staring at the* GIRL)

MAN   *You* stop it, Veronica. We've had all we're going to stand for.

WOMAN   (*Going toward the closet, shoes in hand*)   Hit her and *make* her stop; will you do that, please? Because if *you* won't—
(*The* GIRL *runs toward the door, evading the* MAN *as he grabs at her arm. He catches her from behind as she touches the knob*)

GIRL   *LARRY! LARRY! LARRY!* (*The* WOMAN, *having dropped the shoes, hurries over and helps the* MAN *drag the* GIRL *back to the room's center. She struggles and hits at them*) Let go of me! Let me—*out* of here!

WOMAN   Bitch! Little *bitch!*
(*They struggle further—for several moments, upset-*

ting some bric-a-brac and a chair that the GIRL *grabs
onto—and finally the* GIRL *is thrown to the bed. She
brings herself to a sitting position, winded, trembling, her hair half undone. The* MAN *goes to the
door and locks it. The* WOMAN *sucks at her wrist)*

MAN (*Returning, pocketing the key, his hands shaking*)
You stay there. You don't move from that bed till I say
so. Or else I get the belt. Is that what you want? The
belt?

WOMAN   That's what she *needs,* God damn her. Look at
that!
(*She shows the* MAN *her wrist, and sucks at it
again, glaring at the* GIRL. *The* MAN *tucks his
shirt down into his trousers*)

MAN   Oh, you really take the cake! And it had to be
tonight, didn't it! (*Looks at the* GIRL *as he goes on fixing
himself*) Do you *know* what kind of trouble I've had all
day? We've *all* had all day? Do you *care?* No, *that*
wouldn't interest you; *yourself* is all *you* care about. God
knows you've proved *that* conclusively.

GIRL   I'm not Veronica. You *know* I'm not. (*The* MAN
sighs. The WOMAN *is fixing her hair and her dress*) I'm
Susan Kerner. I'm a junior at B.U. My ID card is in
my bag downstairs.

WOMAN   With *Larry.*
(*The* GIRL *looks at her, and at the* MAN, *who's
righting the upset chair*)

GIRL   It's on the—coatrack or whatever it is. The thing in

the hall, with the antlers. That's where it *was,* anyway.

WOMAN (*To the* MAN, *helping him pick up bric-a-brac*)
I told you to let them have her, didn't I? But oh no,
scandal must never touch the holy name of Brabissant!

MAN   All right, all right.

WOMAN   After *all,* there were Brabissants in Europe who
were actually *street cleaners!* I'm talking about the *suc-
cessful* ones, now.

MAN   Shut up, Nedra.
(*They straighten things; the* GIRL *watches them*)

WOMAN   We could have spared ourselves *all* this *misery*
. . . I won't even *talk* about the *expense.*

GIRL   Who are you?

WOMAN   Tch! "Who are we"!

MAN (*Looks coldly at the* GIRL)   I'm Amos. She's Andy
. . . Now cut it out. Talk like yourself.
(*He goes back to straightening up. The* GIRL
watches)

GIRL   Do you *really believe* I'm—Veronica? Or are you—
playing some kind of game?

WOMAN   You'll find out what kind of "game" we're playing if you don't start talking in your normal voice.
(*The* GIRL *looks about confusedly, and at herself,
and her left arm. She shows the inside of it*)

GIRL   Did Veronica have a scar like this? I was hit by an arrow, in camp, when I was eleven! Camp Allegheny, in Shanksville, Pennsylvania!

WOMAN   You did that yourself, with a pair of scissors. When you were fourteen.

MAN   You've never been to camp.
        (*He and the* WOMAN *do the last of the straightening up. The* GIRL *sings at them, to the tune of "Buffalo Girls"*)

GIRL
        Allegheny girls gonna stand up and fight!
            Gonna stand up and fight!
            Gonna stand up and fight!
        Allegheny girls gonna stand up and fight!
            Gonna fight both night and noon!
        (*The* MAN *and the* WOMAN, *having exchanged commiserating looks and headshakes, are near the door now*)

MAN   You quiet down and get to bed. And in the morning you'd better be talking like yourself.

GIRL (*Standing up*)   Are you out of your *heads?* How long do you think Larry is going to *wait* down there? I'm surprised he hasn't come up *already;* it's been—I-don't-know-*how*-long since he went down—(*Faltering, looking uncertainly at the* MAN *and the* WOMAN)–and he was anxious to—get it over with . . .
        (*Stares at them*)

MAN   Nobody is downstairs.

GIRL   Did you—do something to him?

WOMAN (*To the* MAN)   Will you make her stop this please?

GIRL   You were going to give him Irish whiskey . . . Did you—put something in it?

WOMAN   Why are you *standing here*, Lloyd? Give me the key; *I'll* get the belt!

GIRL (*Withdraws a step*)   My *God*, you're—you're *maniacs* . . . !

WOMAN (*Turning on her*)   *We're* maniacs? Oh that's a *hot* one, coming from *you*, Veronica!

MAN (*Looking at the* GIRL)   Call Dr. Simpson.
      (*Gets the key from his pocket and holds it toward the* WOMAN)

WOMAN (*Looks at the key, and at him*)   Are you *serious*? This is an *act* she's putting on! She doesn't *believe* this Larry business!

MAN (*Turning to her, holding out the key*)   *Call Simpson.*

WOMAN   For God's sake, he was here *twice* already today for Conrad! I'm not going to—

MAN   *Will you for once in your life do what I tell you without giving me arguments, God damn it?* (*Takes her hand and claps the key into it*) Call him! Now!

WOMAN   All right . . . !
   (*Turns to the door and unlocks it*)

MAN   Tell him to hurry.

WOMAN   (*Turns, gives him the key, and glares at him*)
   Two dollars, right down the drain!
      (*She turns, opens the door, and goes out. The* MAN
      *closes the door and locks it. He turns and looks at
      the* GIRL; *she's staring at him fearfully*)

MAN   Get back on the bed.
      (*The* GIRL *withdraws a step. The* MAN *moves
      toward the table by the chaise, pocketing the key.
      He draws a deep breath and massages his forehead.
      The* GIRL, *watching him intently, sits on the edge
      of the bed. The* MAN *takes the glass of milk from
      the table and drinks some of it. He puts it down
      again, and takes a handkerchief from his pocket and
      wipes his mouth, and his forehead, and the palms
      of both his hands*)

GIRL   I thought you . . . loved Veronica . . .

MAN   (*Scrubs a palm thoughtfully*)   We did, long ago,
   and maybe we still could, a little—(*Looks sadly at her*)—
   if you—didn't do things . . .

GIRL   I'm not Veronica. (*The* MAN *sighs*) I'm Susan Kerner. I'm a junior at B.U. (*The* MAN *sits on the foot of
   the chaise. He rubs his face with both hands*) And
   you're not—Veronica's father either. If she was twenty
   in 1935, he must have been—forty, at least. So now
   he'd be—(*Puts a hand to her forehead and closes her*

eyes. To herself) Oh God, thirty-five from seventy-three . . . (*Works it out, lowers her hand*) He'd be almost eighty now. Maybe more. You weren't even that old *before!*

MAN (*Patiently, not looking at her*)   It's 1935. I'm forty-eight. You mother is forty-six.

GIRL (*A pause, watching him*)   I know she is. But she's in Youngstown, Ohio . . . What do you want from me? Do you want me to—pretend I'm Veronica and stay here? Did you—*kill Larry?* Did you? Oh *God,* he'd be *up,* knocking at the door!

MAN (*Sighs, shakes his head and looks at her*)   Don't talk any more, all right? *That's* what I want from you. Don't talk. Let's just wait for Dr. Simpson.
(*He looks away again, deeply troubled. The* GIRL, *watching him, begins pulling the pins from her hair*)

GIRL   There *is* no Dr. Simpson! *He'd* probably be *a hundred* by now! (*Glances at the door*) What is she *really* doing? (*The* MAN *doesn't answer*) Is she changing again? Who's she going to be *now,* Henrietta the cook?

MAN (*Looks at her, holding out a palm-up hand*) You see?

GIRL   She *told* me about Henrietta!

MAN (*Looks away*)   Don't talk. (*The* GIRL, *having removed all the pins, combs her hair down with her fingers. The* MAN *looks at her*) You've let your hair grow . . . (*The* GIRL *glares at him. He looks away again*) It

looks nice, hanging loose that way. Girls *ought* to let their hair grow long.
>   (*A knock at the door brings the* GIRL *instantly to her feet*)

GIRL   *Larry?*

MAN   Sit down.
>   (*He rises and goes toward the door, taking the key from his pocket. The* GIRL *stays standing. The* MAN *unlocks the door and opens it, and the* WOMAN *comes in—as she was before except for a white Band-Aid on her wrist*)

WOMAN   He's coming. (*The* MAN *closes the door and locks it. The* WOMAN *looks at the* GIRL) How's Luise Rainer?

MAN (*Turning, pocketing the key*)   She's not acting. She really thinks it's 1973.

WOMAN   Sure. Tell me another.

GIRL   Turn on the radio. (*The* WOMAN *and the* MAN *look at her*) You have a *radio*, don't you? They were invented by 1935! (*To the* MAN) You said "Amos and Andy" before; they were *radio* stars!

MAN (*Nods*)   We have a radio . . .

GIRL (*A step toward them*)   Then turn it on!
>   (*The* MAN *looks at the* WOMAN)

WOMAN   And how—do you expect us—to get it *up* here?

GIRL (*Snaps her fingers and points at the* WOMAN) Ooooh, you're really quick there, Maureen! Nedra, Henrietta; you improvise *fantastically!* (*Another step toward them, holding out her thumb and forefinger inches apart*) They're going to have radios no bigger than a pack of cigarettes, would you believe that?

MAN   I suppose it's—conceivable . . .

GIRL   You bet your *ass* it's conceivable!
(*She turns and strides across the room and swats at the dresser*)

MAN   No filthy language.

GIRL (*Turning*)   That's *clean* language now!

MAN   Get back on the bed.

GIRL   All right, I will.
(*She turns toward the bed and whips into the bathroom, pulling the door closed. The* MAN *and the* WOMAN *glance at each other, undismayed*)

WOMAN   There's no lock on the door, dear! (*She sits in a chair and makes herself comfortable. The* MAN *sits on the foot of the chaise. After a moment the bathroom door opens and the* GIRL *comes out, looking balefully at them*) We took it out after the *first* time you did that.

GIRL   Now *look* . . . People don't go from sane to crazy just like that. You're pretending. Beautifully, I'll admit, but you're *pretending*.

WOMAN (*To the* MAN) You know, I'm beginning to think you may be right.

MAN I *am*. Look at her, for God's sake.
(*They look at the* GIRL; *she looks at them*)

GIRL We went to a restaurant, Larry and I! (*To the* WOMAN) The Larry you were probably downstairs burying! . . . It was the Golden *something*, I forget the name, but *you* were at the next table, the *two* of you, about sixty years old—it was make-up, I guess—and you were talking with brogues that Saint *Patrick* would have been proud of! . . . You said you were Mr. and Mrs. Mackey, John and Maureen, and you—

WOMAN (*Interrupting her*) John and Maureen?

GIRL Yes! The gardener and the maid!

MAN (*A pause*) We know who they are.

GIRL You said that *I* looked like *Veronica*. We came back here to look at a picture of her. Does any of this ring a bell? Does any of this penetrate the miasma? (*The* MAN *and the* WOMAN *shake their heads, utterly at sea*) You're lying, you've *got* to be . . . On the way here you told us about Cissie, and you asked—

WOMAN (*On her feet*) Don't—you—mention—her—name! (*Going toward the* GIRL, *pointing*) Not from your lips, her name! *Ever!*
(*She stands before the* GIRL, *who retreats a step, frightened. The* MAN *rises*)

MAN *What* did we tell you about her?

GIRL You *know* what you told me, God damn it!
(*A pause*)

MAN What did we tell you?

GIRL (*Retreats farther from the* WOMAN. *To the* MAN)
That she's dying of cancer . . . That she thinks Veronica's alive . . . (*The* WOMAN's *anger is growing. The* GIRL *eyes her uneasily and speaks to the* MAN *again*)
You asked me to pretend to *be* Veronica, to—tell her
I'm not angry with her. She feels guilty about Veronica
having died.

WOMAN (*Claps her hands to her face and cries out*) *Jesus and Mary!* (*A shivering whisper*) Hold me, Lloyd, hold
me; stop me from—hurting her!
(*The* MAN *moves quickly behind the* WOMAN *and
takes her by the shoulders. The* GIRL, *frightened
and confused, looks at her and at the* MAN)

MAN Cissie alive? *Cissie* feeling *guilty?*

GIRL And Veronica dead! That's what you told me!
Tonight! In 1973!

WOMAN (*In an agonized moan*) How can she *say* it . . . ?

MAN (*His lips by her ear, soothingly*) She *believes* it,
Nedra, she *believes* it. Something has—switched over
in her mind; I've heard of that happening, when people
can't face reality.

GIRL (*Shaking her head*) Oh no, no. That *is* reality. That's what you *told* me; in the *restaurant,* in the *car,* in this *room* here. It was—covered with sheets. We had to—fix it all up . . . (*The* WOMAN *lowers her hands and looks at the* GIRL; *the* MAN *looks at her too*) I'm *Susan Kerner* . . .

WOMAN Oh don't you *wish* you were . . . ! (*Peeling the* MAN's *hands from her shoulders*) Don't you wish you were *someone,* anyone, *years* from now, going to school, as free as a bluebird! (*She moves toward the* GIRL; *the* GIRL *retreats*) With a boyfriend Larry to take you to restaurants! And a family somewhere that *loves* you; instead of *this* one, your *own,* that wishes you were *dead!* (*The* GIRL *is retreating around the game table, keeping her distance from the* WOMAN, *who follows*) You think that's reality? That restaurant story? You're really not doing this to torment us?

GIRL It *is* reality. It *happened tonight.*

WOMAN (*Shaking her head*) I'm not going to let you *escape* that easily. I'm going to give you the *real* reality. You're *never* going to switch things around in your mind, not while *I'm* alive! . . . Why do you think you're kept in this room?

GIRL I don't *know* why you're keeping me here!

MAN (*Raising his hand*) You didn't put it right, Nedra. (*Looks at the* GIRL) Why do you think—*Veronica* is kept in this room? *Was* kept in this room, in 1935.

GIRL (*Looks at him for a moment*)   You said—she had
   TB

WOMAN   *TB?*

GIRL   Tuberculosis . . .

WOMAN   If you had TB . . . you would be in a sanitorium
   . . . If you had TB, your door wouldn't be locked, and
   your windows wouldn't be barred. *With wrought iron
   costing six hundred and fifty dollars* . . . If you had TB,
   it would be an enormous improvement.

GIRL   Then—why was she kept here?

WOMAN   You're kept here—because you *killed Cissie* . . .
   Does that "ring a bell"? Does that "penetrate the
   miasma"? (*The* GIRL *shakes her head, staring at the*
   WOMAN) One afternoon when you were fifteen years
   old—Friday, November twenty-first, 1930, to be precise
   —you hit her on the head with a shovel, more than
   once, down in the cellar, and you hauled her into the
   coal bin, and put her beneath the chute. It was the
   day and time when a delivery was coming. It came.
   Five tons. I found her only a little while later; I had
   seen her go down there after you, and one of her legs
   was sticking out. I found *you* up *here,* scrub-a-dub-dub-
   bing. You hadn't quite finished yet, unfortunately for
   you . . . Unfortunately for *me,* your father decided—
   (*A nod to the* MAN)—for his own pea-brained reasons—
   (*And back to the* GIRL)—not to hand you over to the
   police. And he has since spent more than twenty thousand dollars *keeping* our little secret. Five thousand
   dollars to Dr. Harvey, for overlooking the shovel marks

—do you remember Dr. Harvey, before Dr. Simpson? (*The* GIRL *shakes her head*) Another five thousand to the coroner; ditto, ditto, ditto. *Two* thousand dollars to someone at Devereaux, for keeping you on the records through graduation, though we took you out and put you here. You *do* remember Devereaux, don't you? (*The* GIRL *shakes her head*) No? I could have sworn you did. (*Sings, to the tune of "Buffalo Girls"*)

> Devereaux girls gonna stand up and fight,
> > Gonna stand up and fight,
> > Gonna stand up and fight . . .

A thousand dollars every Christmas to John and Maureen—which, I suppose, is why in 1973 they'll be dining in restaurants; five hundred every Christmas to Henrietta; the same to Dr. Simpson, who wondered, of course, why we have a daughter in *stir*; and sundry miscellaneous expenditures—the grillwork, the jigsaw puzzles, the occasional broken mirrors and windows. (*Lifts her wrist, points*) The Band-Aids . . . *That* is reality, Veronica. You killed Cissie. That's why you're kept here in *1935*, and that's why you'll be kept here in *1936*, and in *1937*, and in *1938*, and in *1973*, and in every year until you die. I swore that to Cissie, when I kissed her in her coffin. (*She moves away. The* GIRL *stands shaking her head weakly. The* MAN *sits down again on the foot of the chaise. The* WOMAN *turns to the* GIRL) And you can stop dropping those notes out the window; Conrad won't help you. *He* feels the same way *we* do. When *we* die, *he'll* keep you locked here. *He* swore that to *me*, on the Bible . . . Now what were you saying about meeting us in a restaurant?

GIRL (*Shakes her head weakly, her eyes closed*) I am not

Veronica . . . (*Opens her eyes, looks down at herself*)
This is not my *dress* . . . (*She catches the left sleeve of
it and tears it from the shoulder. The* MAN *spring to his
feet; he and the* WOMAN *hurry to her*) That is not my
puzzle! . . .

> (*They grab her and try to restrain her, but she
> manages to knock part of the puzzle to the floor*)

MAN   Calm down, now! Calm down!

WOMAN   Get her arm!

GIRL   (*Screaming as they hold her*)   This is—*not*—*my*—
ROOM!
> (*A loud knock at the door*)

YOUNG MAN (*Off*)   Say, what's going *on* in there?

GIRL (*A cataract of relief*)   LAAAAREEEEE!
> (*The* MAN *and the* WOMAN *stare at each other*)

YOUNG MAN (*Off*)   Can I come in?
> (*The door is tried*)

GIRL   CALL THE POLICE! GO FIND—(*The* MAN
claps his hand over her mouth but she forces it away)
GO FIND THE PHONE AND CALL THE
POLICE! THEY'RE CRAZY! BOTH OF THEM!
QUICKLY! CALL THE POLICE! THEY'RE IN-
SANE! THEY'VE BEEN—*Let go of me!* (*She breaks
free of the* MAN *and the* WOMAN *and runs to the door*)
CALL THE POLICE, LARRY! CALL THE POLICE!
(*She listens for a moment, then turns and faces the*
MAN *and the* WOMAN, *her hands to her chest*) My God!

My *God!* . . . Did you *hear* him? Or was *that* not reality? (*The* WOMAN *sinks into a chair next to the game
table, her face in her hand. The* MAN *touches her head
soothingly*) He's calling them now. And if your *phone's*
out of order he's getting them *somehow;* he'll run to
the road and flag a car . . . My *God,* you are—very sick
people! I don't even know the *name* for you! You—need
help, very badly! (*Holding her hand out, she goes to the*
MAN, *who's looking mournfully at her*) Now give me
that key *this instant* and *maybe,* just *maybe,* I will not
press charges against you! (*The* MAN *digs the key from
his pocket*) Larry's a lawyer, don't you forget! (*The* MAN
holds out the key; the GIRL *snatches it triumphantly*)
Good *grief,* you almost had me *believing* that *CRAP!*
What kind of kicks did you *get* out of that? I thought
maybe I imagined *everything,* myself, my family, school;
the whole rotten world, God bless it! (*She backs toward
the door*) Camp Allegheny . . . I was even wondering
if I made up little radios! (*Turning, she puts the key
in the door and unlocks it*) Hoo! What a *night* this has
been! *Never again will I talk to strangers!* (*With her
hand on the knob, she turns for a final look at the*
WOMAN, *who has raised her face from her hand and is
looking at the* GIRL *dispassionately*) Oh lady, you are
very, very sick!

> (*She turns and opens the door. The* YOUNG MAN
> *stands there, holding a medical bag and wearing a
> fedora and an open topcoat over a* 1930's *vested
> suit. He has no mustache. The* GIRL *falls back sev-
> eral steps, staring at him. He smiles at her and
> comes into the room, taking off his fedora*)

YOUNG MAN   Veronica . . . (*Nods at the* MAN *and the*
WOMAN) Mr. and Mrs. Brabissant . . . (*The* GIRL *falls*

back farther. The YOUNG MAN *moves to the desk and puts his hat and bag there. He starts taking off his coat)* I rang three or four times, and finally Conrad came down and let me in; I chased him back to bed.

GIRL (*Staring at him*) You son of a bitch . . . it *was* a fake mustache!
 (*He looks at her, startled, and looks at the* MAN, *who is on his way to the door*)

MAN She's been going on that way for half an hour now. (*Closes the door and locks it*)

GIRL And a fake meeting in the restaurant! "Let's go in *here*, Susan, they've got great seafood. Let's sit over there. Hey, don't look now but you're being stared at"! (*To the* WOMAN, *with a brogue*) "Oh don't y' think someone was guidin' our steps tonight, *your* steps 'n *our* steps, bringin' us together"! (*Looking at the* YOUNG MAN *again*) Someone was guiding our steps, all right . . .

YOUNG MAN (*Puts his coat over the back of the desk chair; to the* WOMAN) This doesn't *sound* like an act, Mrs. Brabissant.

MAN (*Pocketing the key*) WOMAN It did before, but
Oh no, this is no act,   I guess she's really—
Doctor; she's absolutely—

GIRL (*Over them, cutting them off*) And our meeting on Sunday! *That* was for this too, wasn't it! You *bastard* . . . And *I* thought *I* picked *you* up, you and your goddamn *dragon kite!*
 (*Pointing overhead*)

YOUNG MAN (*Starting toward her cautiously, smiling, touching his chest*) Veronica, it's *me*, Dr. Simpson . . .

GIRL—Fuck you, you bastard!
(*The* YOUNG MAN *is taken aback; the* MAN *winces painfully; the* WOMAN *smiles*)

WOMAN That's the way they talk in 1973 . . . . Sort of makes you want to die in '72, doesn't it?

YOUNG MAN (*His eyes on the* GIRL *as he approaches her*) Be quiet please, Mrs. Brabissant.
(*The* WOMAN *makes an excuse*-me *face*)

GIRL All right, what kind of *scene* is this? What are you creeps up to?

YOUNG MAN Your parents are worried about you. They asked me to come help you.
(*The* GIRL *looks narrowly at him as he comes nearer*)

GIRL Is Eric involved in this? Is this some kind of *gag*, to make me sorry? Are you a friend of his?

YOUNG MAN "Eric"?

GIRL *Eric Sonneman!*

WOMAN He's downstairs with Larry.
(*The* YOUNG MAN *turns and looks reproachfully at her*)

YOUNG MAN I think you'd better leave the room, Mrs. Brabissant.

WOMAN   I'll be quiet.

YOUNG MAN   No, why don't you go take a look at Conrad?

WOMAN (*Looks at him for a moment*)   I *said*—I'll be quiet.

MAN   Let her stay, Doctor.

YOUNG MAN (*Looks around at the* MAN, *and at the* WOMAN *again, and nods*)   Okay . . . (*Moves closer to the* GIRL) Who's Eric Sonneman?

GIRL   Forget it.

YOUNG MAN   No, come on, tell me; who is he?

GIRL   A better man than you are, Gunga Din.
(*The* YOUNG MAN *looks closely at her, studying her face and her eyes; she turns away*)

YOUNG MAN   It's—1973?

GIRL   From coast to coast.

YOUNG MAN (*Smiling, putting his hand into his jacket pocket*)   Well, at least we're both in America, right? (*Spreads coins on his palm and picks one up, a shiny penny; looks at it*) Nineteen-thirty-four . . . (*He holds it out for the* GIRL *to look at; she turns, glances, and turns away*) Look at it.

GIRL   Collectors—have old coins that are new and shiny.

MAN (*A despondent plea*) Oh Veronica . . .
> (*The* WOMAN *shakes her head and sighs. The*
> YOUNG MAN *puts the penny back on his palm and*
> *examines his other coins*)

YOUNG MAN Nineteen-twenty-eight, 1933, 1931, nine-
teen—
> (*The* GIRL *turns and slams his hand up, knocking*
> *the coins in his face and over his shoulders. He*
> *retreats a step and looks at her*)

WOMAN We've got Band-Aids if you want one.
> (*The* MAN *picks up some of the coins. The* YOUNG
> MAN *still looks at the* GIRL)

YOUNG MAN It looks as if you're beginning to get vio-
lent . . .

MAN (*Straightening up*) She began before you got here.
She tore her dress, we didn't.
> (*A pause, the* YOUNG MAN *and the* MAN *and the*
> WOMAN *looking at the* GIRL. *She points at the*
> YOUNG MAN, *and manages not to sound too fright-*
> *ened*)

GIRL Now you just watch your step, friend. My roommates know I'm out with you.

YOUNG MAN Roommates?

GIRL *Roommates! Roommates!*

YOUNG MAN (*Touching his chest*) Know you're out with
me?

GIRL (*Her assurance leaks away; she eyes him deflatedly*) Who are you? What's your *real* name? (*And now her fright shows*) Jack the Ripper?

YOUNG MAN (*Smiling*) Samuel Simpson, M.D. (*Reaching into his jacket*) Which stands not only for Medical Doctor but also for Massachusetts Driver; I'll show you my license.

GIRL (*Backing a step from him*) Shove it wherever they *used* to shove things.
      (*The* YOUNG MAN *makes a gesture of tolerant assent, puts back his wallet, and crouches and gathers a few coins. The* MAN *gives him the coins he picked up*)

YOUNG MAN Oh. Thanks.

GIRL (*Looks at all of them*) So what happens? Do I get raped? (*Looks at the* WOMAN) By all *three* of you? (*The* WOMAN *glares; the* YOUNG MAN *smiles*)

YOUNG MAN Nobody's going to hurt you, Veronica; we all want—

GIRL (*Interrupting him, going past him*) Oh stop that *Veronica shit*! It's a lie, all of it! You got this house, and you fixed up this room, and you *made up* that whole story! (*To the* MAN *as she passes him*) You're some kind of *freaks*, with a *thing* for 1935!

WOMAN Everything we told you is the truth.

GIRL Bullshit! Why would she have done it? Girls don't

kill their kid sisters. Their *parents* sometimes, like Lizzie Borden, but not their *kid sisters*; I've *never* heard of anything like that!

WOMAN   Let's not go into why you did it, please.

GIRL   Sure not! You forgot to make *up* that part of it! (*Going to her, snapping her fingers*) Come on, Maureen, you're supposed to be the quick one! What's the matter, the old creative power beginning to *wane*?

WOMAN (*Eyes closed; through her teeth*)   Get away from me . . .

GIRL   No, no, come on, you can think of *something*; a lady who comes up like *that* with "How can we get the radio *up* here?"! Come on, why would a fifteen-year-old girl kill her two-years-younger sister? Huh? An argument over a game of Go Fish? (*The* WOMAN *turns away and puts her face to her hand*) Well? Hmm? No ideas? No inspiration?

MAN   *She knew what you were doing with Conrad!* (*The* GIRL *turns and looks at him*) She was *watching* you! Not letting you!

GIRL   Not—letting me?

MAN (*Embarrassed*)   Have—intercourse with him . . . (*The* GIRL *stares at him*) You taught him how, and you made him do it with you, often.

GIRL   He was *twelve* then!

MAN (*Nodding bitterly at her*) Twelve, yes, twelve. Your brother.

GIRL *Veronica's* brother . . .

WOMAN *Your* brother . . .
(*She has raised her face from her hand and is looking hatefully at the* GIRL's *back*)

MAN Cissie caught you with him, in the garage, a few days before. You begged her not to tell us, you swore you would stop. She agreed to keep quiet, to spare *us,* but she—kept watch on you. That's why she followed you into the cellar. That's why you *meant* her to follow you . . . Conrad told us that night. He was glad to get free of you. You had—terrorized him.
(*He and the* GIRL *look at each other. The* YOUNG MAN *looks at the floor, shaking his head. The* WOMAN *watches the* GIRL, *who moves toward the* MAN)

GIRL I take back what I said . . . *You* are the quick one! That's *beautiful!* It fits in—like a piece of that puzzle! Forget about your mill; you can start writing soap operas! And by the way, don't worry: the Depression's going to get better; Roosevelt is going to fix the whole thing!

YOUNG MAN (*Smiling*) That's what they say. Let's keep our fingers crossed.

GIRL All *right*, we'll go through it *again.* (*Going to the* YOUNG MAN, *chanting in a patient singsong*) It's 1973, it is not 1935. I'm Susan Kerner, I'm not Veronica. I

go to B.U. I come—(*Turning, going toward the* MAN)—
from Youngstown, Ohio. My father's a dentist, room two
hundred in the Hoover Building. My mother studied
singing with *Rosa Ponselle*; she sings at—(*Turning, going toward the* WOMAN)—parties, it's hard to stop her.
I have a brother Sandy who's traveling in Portugal.
Come home, Sandy! (*The* MAN *and the* YOUNG MAN
look at each other; the MAN *nods*) We live at Eight
Winthrop Circle and our phone number's new but I'll
think of it in a second. I live here on (*Turning, going
toward the* YOUNG MAN *again; speaking faster now as if
she might wind into madness*)—Exeter with *two* roommates! Diane who's a dum-dum and Leslie who's heaven!
(*The* YOUNG MAN, *with the* GIRL *coming toward him,
looks at the* WOMAN; *she head-signs toward the desk*) I
have a paper on ethnicity that's due on Monday and
all I've done is gather material! (*Turning, going toward
the* MAN) Nixon's in the White House—(*Arms wide,
triumphantly*)—*Richard M. NIXON!* (*Pointing back
at the* YOUNG MAN, *who was about to move*) George
McGovern! (*She goes on toward the* MAN. *The* YOUNG
MAN *goes toward the desk*) Teddy Kennedy! *Ethel* Kennedy! *Jackie* Kennedy! Ari Anassis! (*Turning, going
toward the* WOMAN) The Rolling Stones! The Mothers
of Invention! Mama Cass! Johnny Cash! Henry Kissin-
ger! (*The* YOUNG MAN *is at the desk, his back turned*)
Dan Rather! Margaret Mead! R. D. Laing! Robert Red-
ford! Robert Goulet! Robert *Stack!* Robert *anyone!*
Gloria Steinem! Jane Fonda! Paul Newman! (*Turning*)
Joanne Woodward! Woody Allen! (*She looks around.
The* WOMAN *rises*) Woody Guthrie! Woody—*WOOD-
PECKER!* (*She sees the* YOUNG MAN *as he turns from
the desk, his right hand behind his back*) What have
you got there?

YOUNG MAN (*Moving toward her harmlessly*) Nothing to
hurt you. Just to calm you down.

MAN (*Moving toward her too*)   What were all those
names you were saying?
>(*She stares at them, then turns and runs to the
dresser, grabs a piece of bric-a-brac and throws it at
the* YOUNG MAN; *it smashes on the wall. She grabs
another but the* MAN *catches her by her left arm
and pulls her around, and the thrown object flies
toward the bookcase. The* YOUNG MAN *runs over
and locks the* GIRL's *right arm under his left*)

GIRL   Let go! Let go of me! (*To the* YOUNG MAN) *No
needle! No needle!* (*A hypodermic syringe is in the
YOUNG MAN's right hand. He and the* MAN *drag the
GIRL toward the chaise*) No! No! No! No! All right! All
right! All right! All right, all right. All right. I'm Veronica. I'm Veronica. (*The* WOMAN *has gone quickly to
the chaise, and as the* YOUNG MAN *and the* MAN *bring
the* GIRL *to it, she snatches away the decorative pillow*)
I'm Veronica. I'm Veronica. I'm Veronica. I'm Veronica.
(*The* YOUNG MAN *and the* MAN *get her onto the chaise
and stand half-crouching on either side of it, holding
her by her arms. The* WOMAN *comes around to the
YOUNG MAN's side, the pillow in her hand*) I'm Veronica. I'm Veronica. I'll calm down. I don't need any—
needle. Really. I'm Veronica. I'm all right. I'll—stop pretending. You were right—Mother—I was only pretending. I'll stop though. I won't do it any more. (*The
WOMAN and the MAN watch her intently; the* YOUNG
MAN, *syringe poised, watches them and her*) I'll—try to
talk in my normal voice—(*With a Massachusetts accent, trembling with fright*)—but I'm hoarse now and

I probably won't sound like myself anyway. But I'm all right. I'll calm down. I'll go to bed quietly the way you said I should—Father. I'm—sorry I made so much trouble. I was—jealous because Conrad is getting all the attention. With his fever I mean. I'm sorry. (*Tries to make a smile*) I'm all right. You can let me go now. I'll get undressed and go to bed.

WOMAN (*Looks at her for a long cold moment*)   Do you remember now why we keep you here?

GIRL   Yes. Yes, I do! I never forgot, I was only pretending.

WOMAN   *Why* do we keep you here?

GIRL   Because I—killed—
       (*Stops warily, looking at the* WOMAN)

WOMAN   Say it, say her name . . .

GIRL (*A hesitant pause*)   Cissie . . . I killed Cissie. I'm sorry, Mother. I swear I am!

MAN   And you know *why* you killed her?

GIRL   Because she knew what I was doing with Conrad. And she—wasn't letting me do it—any more. (*Looks pleadingly at the* MAN, *and at the* WOMAN, *and at the* YOUNG MAN, *who has lowered the syringe. To all of them*) You see? I've stopped pretending. I'm Veronica. It's 1935. I—made up all those names, and those things about Susan. There *is* no Susan. I made it all up. Everything . . . Will you let go of me now? Please? I'll

73

go to bed and I won't make any trouble. Tomorrow I'll
—paint, and work on my puzzle. My voice will be back
to normal. I'll stop dropping notes out the window. I'll
be—good from now on.

WOMAN   That's what you said the last time. When you
pretended you were French, and wouldn't speak Eng-
lish.

GIRL (*A small pause*) This time I *mean* it, Mother. I
swear I do.
  (*The* MAN *releases the* GIRL's *arm and stands
  straight. The* YOUNG MAN *releases her other arm
  and puts the syringe on the lamp table. The* GIRL
  rubs her arms, watching the WOMAN, *who turns
  away, looks at the pillow in her hands, and looks
  to heaven*)

WOMAN   Oh *God*, Lloyd, what are we going to *do* with
her?

MAN (*Shaking his head, looking at the* GIRL)   I don't
know, Nedra, I honestly don't know . . .

WOMAN (*Turning to the* GIRL)   You *say* you won't do this
again, but there's so much—*evil* in you, how can you
not try to—lie it away?

GIRL   I won't. I promise. Never again.

MAN   Cissie was an *angel*, and you murdered her . . .

GIRL (*Nodding*) Yes . . . yes . . .

74

WOMAN   *Conrad* was an angel too, until you—did what you did with him.

GIRL   Yes . . .

MAN   We were a good family, a *fine* one, no matter *what* your mother says—and now we can't even have guests in the house, because of you!

WOMAN   *You've* locked *us* in, damn you! *We're* the prisoners, not you!

GIRL   (*A pause, and a hesitant suggestion*)   Then—why not—let me go away? I'll go far away, and I—won't bother you. I'll—change my name . . .
    (*A pause*)

YOUNG MAN   *There's* an idea, Mrs. Brabissant . . .

WOMAN   (*Turns away, shaking her head, her eyes closed*)   No, no, we can't let you go . . . I swore to Cissie . . .

GIRL   Angels forgive . . .

WOMAN   Not you, they don't . . . Not a girl who takes her twelve-year-old brother into the garage, and plays with him—(*Turning toward the* GIRL)—and shows herself, and makes him touch, and kiss . . . ! Not a girl who leads her sister into the cellar, and hits with a shovel, and hits, and hits, and *hits!* And hauls her into the coal bin, and *waits,* and *watches! Nobody* forgives *you,* Veronica! Not even *angels!* Not even *Jesus!* (*She goes toward the* GIRL, *who would flee the chaise, but the men catch her arms again and keep her there*) We *kill* you, we don't *forgive* you! *We kill you!*

(*The* GIRL *screams, a half-scream stopped by the pillow that the* WOMAN *presses to her face. The* WOMAN *sits on the side of the chaise and holds the pillow across the* GIRL'*s face with both hands. The men hold the* GIRL'*s straining arms. Her head moves from side to side, but the* WOMAN *holds the pillow tightly across it. The* GIRL *moans muffledly; her legs kick. The* MAN *catches them around the knees, holds them, and struggles one-handed with her left arm. The* YOUNG MAN, *restraining the* GIRL'*s right arm easily with both hands, watches the* WOMAN'*s face with interest. The* GIRL'*s moaning and straining grow more desperate. A while passes and they begin to weaken. Nothing else changes. Another while passes, a long one, and the* YOUNG MAN *puts the* GIRL'*s arm down to the floor. He stands straight and rubs the small of his back, still watching the* WOMAN'*s face. The* MAN *lets go of the* GIRL'*s legs and arm, watches the pillow and the* WOMAN'*s hands for another moment, and touches the* WOMAN'*s shoulder. He stands straight and massages his upper arms. The* YOUNG MAN *loosens the knot of his tie and unbuttons his collar. The* WOMAN *takes the pillow slowly from the* GIRL'*s face; its eyes and mouth are open, unmoving. The* WOMAN *rises, looks at the* GIRL *for a moment, and moves away. She flings the pillow away and lifts her arms in a gesture of relief and liberation. The* YOUNG MAN *crouches, slides his arms in under the* GIRL'*s back and knees, and lifts her from the chaise. He carries her around the foot of it and toward the bed. The* MAN *watches the* WOMAN *hopefully. The* YOUNG MAN *spills the* GIRL *onto the bed, rolling her off his arms so that she falls face down. He*

turns and looks at the MAN *and the* WOMAN, *con-*
temptuously, then draws back his sleeve and looks
at his watch. He goes to the WOMAN *and tries to*
put the watch before her face but she turns away.
He taps at the watch with an insistent finger)

YOUNG MAN   *Six minutes of eleven* . . . (*He brings the*
watch, still tapping at it, to the MAN, *who looks angrily*
at him) Ten-fifty-four. (*Histrionically*) A new record!
But *fated—to be broken!* (*To the* WOMAN) When is
the next one going to end? *Twelve, twenty, nine?* (*To*
the MAN) *Three, oh, seven?*

MAN   There isn't going to be a next one. This is the last.
We all agreed. Didn't we? (*The* YOUNG MAN *turns*
away scornfully and, with a fingerstroke, rips his vest
unbuttoned. The WOMAN *stands silently, her eyes*
closed) It's the last. We agreed. (*He stands uncertainly*
for a moment, then goes and takes the decorative objects
from the bookcase. The YOUNG MAN *stands rubbing the*
back of his neck angrily. The MAN *brings the objects*
toward the desk) Well don't just stand there, boy, get
the dress off her.

YOUNG MAN (*Starts toward the bed, stops, turns back*)   I
am too TIRED to get the dress off her! (*The* MAN,
with a sigh, opens a desk drawer and puts the objects
into it. The YOUNG MAN *moves nearer the* WOMAN,
mimicking broadly with a thick brogue) "Oh we usually
go t' a restaurant on State Street, where John has a
cousin who's a waiter, an' we don't have t' tip, praise the
Lord, an' it's such a big *savin'* for us!"

WOMAN (*Turns and looks acidly at him for a moment*)   I

wouldn't have had to go through all that if *you* hadn't been working *against* us! *That's* what gets worse every time, *you*, not *us*! The way you *needle* and *tease* and ask *questions* you're not *supposed* to ask!

YOUNG MAN (*Looks at her*) Oh . . . (*Gently, still with a brogue*) Well y' see dear, the reason I do that is it gives me an excuse to look at y' as if I don't like y' too much. 'Cause I'm not a good enough actor to pretend that I think you're charmin' and lovable.

MAN All right, boy, shut your mouth and get the dress off her!
(*The* YOUNG MAN, *still angry, goes toward the bed. The* MAN, *gathering objects from the table near the chaise, watches the* WOMAN *as she moves toward the foot of it. She sits, and he turns and goes toward the desk. In the next minutes he returns all the room's decorative objects to the drawers from which they were taken in Act One*)

YOUNG MAN (*Holding the* GIRL *toward her side, unfastening her belt*) That whole first part has gotten too goddamned elaborate! (*The brogue again*) "Here's where she made her pins an' bracelets. Here's her wire, here's her colored glass." How come you don't give a goddamn PIN-*making demonstration* while you're at it!
(*He undoes the back of the dress. The* MAN *pays him no heed. The* WOMAN *pulls her hair off; a wig. Beneath it is the hair she had in Act One; she fluffs it out. The* YOUNG MAN *starts taking the dress off the* GIRL)

WOMAN   I didn't notice you rushing your doctor business any . . .
>   (*The* YOUNG MAN *turns and comes angrily toward her*)

YOUNG MAN   What do you *want* me to do? Come in and say "Hello, Veronica, I'm Dr. Simpson; look at this needle I'm going to stick in your arm"? Is *that* what you want? Just say the word; it's fine with *me*! *I* don't need all this—(*A gesture around him as he seeks words*) —this *Walpole Drama Society*! (*Moves closer to her*) All I need—*darlin*'—is what's there on the bed, and I'd like to get to it *early* enough so that I can *stay awake* when I've *got* it!
>   (*The* WOMAN *turns the wig on her hand and picks at it as the* YOUNG MAN *lets that sink in*)

MAN (*Busy at the bookcase*)   Will you *get on with it*, boy?
>   (*The* YOUNG MAN *goes back to the bed and resumes taking off the* GIRL's *dress. The* WOMAN *toys with the wig*)

YOUNG MAN   All right, fine! Next time the doctor part is going to take two seconds; you just *see* if she says what you want her to say!

MAN   There's not going to be any next time.
>   (*Goes toward the bathroom, his hands full of bric-a-brac fragments*)

WOMAN   Save those pieces. Maybe I can glue it back together.

MAN (*Stops, turns toward her*) I don't *think* so . . .
>(*The* YOUNG MAN *slaps the dress around a bedpost*)

WOMAN Well, I want to *try*. Put them there.
>(*The* MAN *puts the fragments doubtfully on the game table, clear of the puzzle. He brushes his hands off and looks around. All the decorative objects have been put away*)

YOUNG MAN (*Taking off the* GIRL's *slip; grudgingly*) There's a new *silicone cement* that's supposed to be good.

WOMAN There is? (*He doesn't respond. The* MAN *takes the dress from the bedpost and finds its tear*) Do you know where to get it?

YOUNG MAN No. These *her* panties?

WOMAN Yes.

MAN (*Showing the* WOMAN *the dress*) You want to sew this, don't you?

WOMAN (*Taking it*) Mm-hmm.
>(*He reaches for the wig; she gives it to him. He goes toward the door, getting the key from his pocket. The* YOUNG MAN *rolls the* GIRL's *stockings down her legs. The* MAN *unlocks the door and opens it. The* WOMAN *fingers the dress in her lap. The* MAN, *pocketing the key, goes to the desk and picks up the coat, the hat, and the medical bag. The* YOUNG MAN *unhooks the* GIRL's *bra and bends one of her arms from its strap. The* MAN *goes out.*

The YOUNG MAN *moves from the bed and calls after him)*

YOUNG MAN   Hey, open my door while you're out there, will you? (*He watches for a moment, then goes back to the bed and finishes taking off the* GIRL's *bra, raising her middle to pull it from under her. He gathers the slip and stockings and tosses them with the bra into the bathroom. Moving to the side of the bed, he rolls the* GIRL *toward him onto her back, crouches, and picks her up. He turns, holding her in his arms, and moves toward the* WOMAN. *She fingers the dress, not turning. He stands looking at her for a moment)* Sure an' it's a good night I'm wishin' y', Mrs. Mackey. May the good Lord bless an' keep y'.

(*He carries the* GIRL *to the doorway, angles her through, and carries her out. The* WOMAN *fingers the dress, frowning. She looks in her mid-fifties now. She lifts the dress from her lap—and puts it behind her. She rubs her cheek, looks at her fingertips, rubs them with her thumb. The* MAN *comes in with the bundle of dust covers. He too now seems in his mid-fifties. He puts the bundle on the floor and spreads it apart, glancing uncertainly at the* WOMAN)

MAN   It—spoiled things a little, didn't it, her saying all those names.

WOMAN (*Nods*)   A little . . .

MAN (*Drawing loose a cover*)   It was nice her being able to do the accent though. I thought that was a big help.

(*The* WOMAN *nods. The* MAN *begins covering a chair nearby*) She *looked* good too.

WOMAN (*Turning, surprised*)   Did you think so?

MAN   Yes, definitely. She had the right eyes, the line of the jaw . . .

WOMAN (*Waving a hand, turning away again*)   No . . .

MAN (*Returning to the bundle*)   Yes! Not like the *first* one, of course. My *God,* we'll *never* find another one like *her!* That was *uncanny!* I mean—we *wouldn't* find another one like her. If we were going to *do* another.
(*He draws another cover from the bundle. The* WOMAN *looks at him.*)

WOMAN   Did I really terrorize you?

MAN   What do you mean?

WOMAN   That's what you said. "Conrad was glad to get free of you. You had terrorized him." And you said it with such feeling . . .

MAN   I was speaking like Father then, saying what *he* would have said.

WOMAN   Did you tell *them* I terrorized you?

MAN (*Dropping the cover and going to her*)   I never used the word in my whole life, until tonight. I don't even know what put it into my head. (*Crouching beside her*) If you had "terrorized" me, I wouldn't have let you out of here, would I? I would have kept you locked in here after they died, the way I swore I would.

WOMAN (*Smoothing his hair*)   We *both* wanted it, didn't we? From the very beginning? It wasn't only *my* doing . . .

MAN   No, no, of course it wasn't! You didn't "terrorize" me, Veronica, honest to God you didn't! (*They kiss each other lovingly. The* MAN *smiles at the* WOMAN) I got carried away being Father, that's all!

WOMAN   You were so like him tonight! I expected you to take out one of his *cigars* any minute!

MAN   You were Mother to a T! It was *fantastic!*

WOMAN (*With her "Maureen" brogue*)   And how about John and Maureen? Didn't we do them just wonderfully, darlin'?

MAN (*With his "John" brogue*)   Sure an' it's regular actors we are! Or could have been, if—if we'd *had* to be somethin'. (*Rises from his crouching position and drops the brogue, suddenly grave*) Come on. Let's get out of here.
     (*Backs from the* WOMAN)

WOMAN   Conrad.

MAN   What?

WOMAN (*Rising*)   It really happened tonight. The way I always hoped it would. When she admitted everything, when you and Boy were holding her there, she was *me* all of a sudden, and I was—me and yet *not me.* And after she was punished, I felt so *free,* and so *clean!* As if I'd never done a single thing wrong in my entire life!

MAN   Good! Good!

WOMAN   And then *Boy* had to ruin it all, shouting at me, bringing everything back . . .

MAN (*Moving to her again*)   God damn him!

WOMAN   We should have got rid of him the day he was born. I wanted to, remember? But you wouldn't let me.

MAN   A *baby*, Veronica!

WOMAN   Do you know what he told this girl? What *she* told *me*? That I didn't *touch* him enough! As if *touching* him would have made any difference!

MAN   But it *worked* tonight and we're done! We can close up this room forever!

WOMAN   It *didn't* work! He ruined it! I want to do *one more*, with him not having anything to do with it! We'll get the girl ourselves. We can do it. John and Maureen can . . . (*Looking past him toward an imaginary girl, speaking with her brogue again*) Oh darlin', excuse us for starin' at y', but you're the spittin' image of this girl we used to know a long, long time ago!

MAN   We're not going to do another! You said this would be the last!

WOMAN The *next* one will be the last! I swear it will!

MAN You *always* swear that!

WOMAN But we know it can *work* now, if *he* doesn't ruin it! And I've *got* to make it work, Conrad!

MAN She won't *admit* anything unless Boy is here holding the needle over her!

WOMAN Oh yes she will . . . (*With the brogue again, and focused again on the imaginary girl*) She'll admit *everythin'*. What she done to poor Cissie, what she done with Conrad . . . The Mister and Missus'll get her to admit, sooner or later, and when *that* one's gone, she'll be gone forever.

MAN We're not going to do another one, Veronica. We agreed. Come on, it's late. (*Kisses her cheek*) Let's get to bed now.
    (*He moves away from her and begins quickly turning out lamps. She stays focused on the girl*)

WOMAN Veronica was her name. Y' could be her *twin* practically! Oh, how her father and mother loved her! Was all the time touchin' her! Kids—should be touched a *lot*, y' know.
    (*The* MAN *is near the door, watching her with anguish*)

MAN Come out. Come out now . . .

WOMAN (*Looks at herself, at the room*) I can't. I'm still locked in here.

85

MAN (*Hurrying to her*) No, no, no, no, you're not! She's gone! She's dead! The door is open! Look! I unlocked it for you!
>(*He takes her in his arms and kisses her. She stiffens in the embrace and pushes free*)

WOMAN Let—go of me! (*Retreats, confused*) How can you *kiss* me that way? I—I don't even know who you are! (*She retreats farther; they stare at each other*) Do you—*really* think I'm Veronica? Or is this some kind of *game* you're playing? We were—in the Golden *something*, Larry and I. *You* were at the next table, talking with a brogue . . . You said you were John Mackey . . .

MAN Veronica . . . !

WOMAN *My ID card is in my bag downstairs!* Get Larry up here!

MAN (*Stares at her*) What Larry . . . ?

WOMAN Larry Eastwood! The man I came here with! Get him up here! And bring me my clothes! I want to go now!

MAN (*Going to her*) What are you *doing*, Veronica?

WOMAN I'm not Veronica! This is not my dress! This is not my puzzle! (*Sweeps the bric-a-brac fragments from the game table to the floor*) This is not my ROOM!

MAN All right! All right! (*Backs hastily, fearfully, toward the door*) I'll get your clothes! I'll get everything! Be quiet!

WOMAN   What kind of scene is this? What are you creeps up to? (*The* MAN *hurries out and closes the door. The sound of the bolt is heard. The* WOMAN *stares at the closed door*) It's—1973. It's not—1935. (*She looks around the room, and at the barred window where the curtain lifts in a breeze*) Oh my *God* . . . ! (*She runs to the door and beats at it*) Mother? Father? Let me out! Please unlock the door, Mother! Please! Let me out of here!

(*As the curtain quickly falls*)

47446